50 Simple Things You Can Do To Raise A Child Who Loves Math

50 Simple Things You Can Do To Raise A Child Who Loves Math

Kathy A. Zahler, M.S.

Macmillan • USA

*for Olivia, her cousin Althea,
and her friends Rosie, Gareth, Amane, Colden, and Isabel . . .
and for all the other children who are just discovering the world.*

*Many thanks to Chantal Dietemann
for her anxiety-free assistance.*

Macmillan Reference • USA
A Simon & Schuster Macmillan Company
1633 Broadway
New York, NY 10019-6785

Macmillan Publishing books may be purchased for business or sales
promotional use. For information please write: Special Markets Department,
Macmillan Publishing USA, 1633 Broadway, New York, NY 10019.

Manufactured in the United States of America

10   9   8   7   6   5   4   3   2   1
Library of Congress Number: 96-079997
ISBN: 0-02-861766-5

Contents

Section 2   Modify Children's Behavior

Section 3   Modify Your Own Behavior

Section 4   Focus on Specific Skills

Introduction

To the Parents

If a child is to keep alive his inborn sense of wonder. . . he needs the companionship of at least one adult who can share it, rediscovering with him the joy, excitement and mystery of the world we live in.

—Rachel Carson

I love to watch my daughter and her friends play. They can find boundless pleasure in locating a clover among leaves of grass or balancing a rock on end. Their explorations mirror my own childhood explorations, and my parents before me, and theirs before them. Every child rediscovers the world as if it had never been charted before. Serving as witness to that rediscovery is one of the greatest joys of parenthood.

I have to admit that I did not grow up loving math. I entered school fascinated by math and left school years later avoiding and fearing it. I rediscovered my childhood love for math by teaching it to children.

There are many reasons we lose the "inborn sense of wonder" that makes the world of numbers so vibrant and exciting. Bad teaching, personal biases, and a failure to relate the math of school to "real life" turn far too many of us from math lovers to math haters. It doesn't have to be that way.

This book has five sections. The first is called "Make Math Connections." Most parents and all teachers have heard the mournful cry, "Why do I need to know this?" This section helps you show your child when math is used in "real life." You'll connect math concepts and skills to setting the table, playing cards, planning trips, doing chores, and other daily activities.

The next two sections have to do with your child's actions and your own attitudes. "Modify Children's Behavior" includes ideas for overcoming some stumbling blocks to math success. "Modify Your Own Behavior" shows you how to improve your child's capabilities by changing the way you think and act. Could your own biases about math be impeding your child's achievement?

Mastery of certain math skills is vital, and that is the focus of the fourth and fifth sections. "Focus on Specific Skills" covers important areas in problem solving, mental arithmetic, and spatial visualization. I review each concept briefly and offer ideas for you to use with your child to reinforce skills painlessly and easily. The initial problems are for you, the parent. They allow you to see everyday, adult applications of the concepts your children are learning in school. Answers to problems, when they appear, are underlined. The suggestions at the end of each chapter are for you to use with your children. They range in difficulty from easy (for children from preschool through primary grades) to challenging (for older kids).

Many children move along quite contentedly and successfully in math only to hit a wall between third and fourth grades, when certain higher-level math concepts kick into gear. "Focus on Difficult Concepts" is a section for you to use with your older children—fourth grade and up. These concepts—fractions, percents, ratios and proportions, negative numbers, and probability—often give even math lovers trouble. I've included some activities that may allow you to preview skills with younger children as well.

As you skim the pages of this book, you will find a variety of activities to do with your child. Pick and choose the activities that best match your child's ability level and interests. Don't feel limited by my words; you and your child should determine where the activity will take you. There is no "right way" to explore.

You are your child's first teacher and the adult most likely to share his or her explorations. Your good example now and later in your child's school career can counteract those experiences that tend to stunt a child's sense of wonder. In the process of helping your child, you may rediscover for yourself "the joy, excitement and mystery of the world we live in."

Kathy A. Zahler

SECTION 1

Make
Math Connections

1.

Suggest Practical Reasons for Math:
Shopping

> Gregory was struggling through his third page of homework problems when he threw his hands up in despair.
>
> "Why do I have to learn this stuff? I'm never going to use it!" he wailed.
>
> His mother came in to see what he was fussing about. "Are you kidding?" she asked after skimming the page. "I use this 'stuff' all the time. Subtracting money, finding percents—come with me to the grocery store this week, and I'll show you."

A common complaint of schoolchildren is that the material they're being taught is so obscure and meaningless that it bears no relation to anything they'll use in "real life." Although there are a few math concepts that are truly hard to justify—dividing negative numbers, for example—most of math is practical if you just make the application clear. It's often hard to see the application when you're faced with page after page of written problems. Parents can help by sharing real-life math with their children.

Grocery shopping is full of math possibilities. Shoppers compare prices, recognize money values, subtract the values of coupons, determine percent off, estimate totals, and so on. Do you have enough money? That's a math problem. Is this a better buy than that? That's a math problem, too.

How to Practice Math on a Shopping Trip

Show children how to read unit price tags, and point out the various units of measure, such as price per ounce and price per sheet. Assign children certain products from your grocery list—paper towels, corn flakes, and frozen peas, for example—and have them locate the best buy for each product.

Ask children to compare their favorite cereal or juice brand with other brands and determine which is the better buy.

Have children select meat packages that contain enough for a meal for your entire family.

As you wait in line, put children in charge of the coupons and ask them to determine how much you will save.

Ask children to look for "two for the price of one" and "buy one, get one free" sale items and determine how much you can save over the regular price or over the price of two "best buy" products of the same type.

Have children help you weigh items such as vegetables, nuts, and grains. Ask them to estimate the cost of the amount they weighed.

Have children estimate the number of bags it will take to hold your purchases. Compare their guess with the actual total. Could the bags have been packed more efficiently?

✐ Have children use labels and price tags to find the cost of a single serving of cereal or a sandwich's worth of bread. How much does it cost for breakfast or lunch for a week?

✐ At department or clothing stores, ask children to determine the cost of a coveted item if they wait to buy until it's marked down 20, 40, or 50 percent.

✐ Have children look at the register total and the amount you give the clerk and quickly determine how much change you should receive.

When you get home, talk about why it is important to you to be a careful consumer, and point out that knowing a little math goes a long way toward avoiding rip-offs and making sensible purchases. Review the many times you used math on your excursion and the ways in which it saved you money.

2.

Suggest Practical Reasons
for Math: Cooking

 My husband looks up from the bread machine with a scowl. "Why does it have to be 2 cups plus 1 tablespoon? Who decided that a single tablespoon could make all the difference?"

As anyone who has used a bread machine knows, getting the ingredients exactly right and in the right order is a matter of utmost importance. We ran through several bricklike loaves and one that resembled sawdust before investing in a new set of measuring cups and vowing to follow recipes to the letter.

My husband once taught a science course based entirely around cooking. The laws of thermodynamics, properties of matter, and mixing solutions all come into play as you make a casserole for dinner. Cooking is a great introduction to a number of math principles as well.

If you have spent any time in the kitchen, certain things are probably second nature by now. You don't need to think very hard to divide a package of hamburger into patties for your family, and you have a pretty good idea how long to cook an egg. For a child, however, many of these skills are brand-new and fascinating.

How to Practice Math While Cooking Dinner

Put out your measuring utensils. Have children locate each correct utensil and measure the ingredients as you read from a recipe. Challenge older children to do all the measuring with only a 1-cup measuring cup and a teaspoon. (See the conversion chart on the following page.)

Have children help you convert a recipe for four to a recipe for eight (or for older children, a recipe for six), changing each measurement as needed. Similarly, convert a recipe for eight to a recipe for four. This is one task where multiplication and division of fractions meets a real-life application.

Example:

Swordfish with Salsa

(serves 4)	× 2	=	(serves 8)
4 swordfish steaks	× 2	=	8 swordfish steaks
2 T olive oil	× 2	=	4 T olive oil
2 cloves garlic	× 2	=	4 cloves garlic
1 jalapeño pepper	× 2	=	2 jalapeño peppers
5 Italian tomatoes	× 2	=	10 Italian tomatoes
$\frac{1}{2}$ cup cilantro	× 2	=	1 cup cilantro

Have young children keep track of the time as you wait for a cake to bake or a casserole to heat. Instead of setting a timer, put the children in charge of telling you when the food is ready.

Here's one that I always have trouble with: Plan a party meal with your children and determine how much time each course of the meal takes to prepare. Have children design a timeline showing when you should start each task to ensure that everything is ready on time.

Example:

<—5:15————5:30————5:45————6:00————6:15—>
chop onions   start sauce   make salad   cook pasta   toss salad

 Let children (carefully!) read the poultry or candy thermometer.

Have children point out where to slice pizza or a pan of brownies to obtain a given number of equal-sized pieces.

Measurement Conversion Chart

Liquid	Dry
8 ounces = 1 cup	3 teaspoons = 1 tablespoon
2 cups = 1 pint	2 tablespoons = 1 ounce
4 cups = 1 quart	16 tablespoons = 1 cup
2 pints = 1 quart	16 ounces = 1 pound
4 quarts = 1 gallon	

3.

Suggest Practical Reasons for Math: Home Repair

I once had brand-new windows installed in the kitchen of a very old house. The installer worked by the book, using a level to make sure the windows were true. Unfortunately, the house itself was several degrees from horizontal, having settled over a century and a half, and the finished product looked completely askew. Had the windows been hung parallel with the floor, they would not have opened properly. Rather than risk seasickness every time I entered the kitchen, I begged my window man to plane the angles of the window frames to make the windows appear to match the lines of the kitchen. It took a good eye and a number of mathematical calculations for him to complete the task, but the result was a miracle of trompe l'oeil window hanging.

From a very young age, children show an eagerness to manipulate objects, and studies of the brain clearly show that this manipulation is vital to a child's development. Nobody grasps the concept of *long* and *short* without first seeing or feeling the difference between an object that is long and one that is short. Even your youngest children can learn some basic math concepts while helping you with home-repair chores.

How to Practice Math While Repairing the Home

Have young children help you organize your toolbox by sorting screws, bolts, nuts, and washers by size and shape. (Be sure the children are not too young—you don't want them still at an age when they're putting everything in their mouths.) Younger children can also have a good time and learn something about comparative measurement by organizing a set of crescent wrenches in increasing size order.

Show children how to use the measuring tools in your toolbox, from T squares to tape measures to levels. Put children in charge of measuring and marking as you work. (You may want to check their work; "measure twice, cut once" is a good rule to follow.)

Allow older children to use your scrap wood and other leftover materials to design and build something themselves.

Ask children to use their own bodies as an estimation tool for big projects. For example, "If you are 4 feet tall, about how long a sheet of wallpaper will reach from floor to ceiling?" and "If your finger span is 5 inches, about how long will a dowel need to be to fit between these rails?"

Contrast situations in which exact measurement is vital to the task to situations in which estimation is fine. Point out tasks for which you must add a little to an exact measurement (cutting screen for a screen door) or subtract a little from an exact measurement (placing picture hangers).

Have children identify parallel lines, perpendicular lines, and angles (right, acute, and obtuse) in the work you are doing. Discuss the way angles fit together in a mitered window frame, the way two walls and a ceiling form three right angles, and how pipes or ducts are set parallel to one another in the basement.

4.

Suggest Practical Reasons for Math: Crafts

I learned to crochet from a left-handed aunt. She taught me the movements, and I imitated her precisely. I learned the technique, but for reasons I can't determine, I was completely unable to transpose the movements to my right hand. So when I crochet, which I do slowly and awkwardly, I hold the work in my right hand and the needle in my left. It's a craft based on patterns and geometry, and my patterns will forever be backward.

Crafts generally involve measurement, design, patterns, and spatial visualization. Because crafts often require children to follow step-by-step directions, they are an excellent learning tool. You needn't shove a hobby down your child's throat; usually children find their way toward hobbies they enjoy through trial and error. However, there's nothing wrong with sharing a hobby you love.

Whether you are building birdhouses, weaving pot holders, or throwing pots, crafts provide opportunities to introduce or reinforce math skills. Very young children can explore shapes and sizes by helping you on a quilting project. Older children can help you mark measurements as you create a work of art from wood. Here are some ideas for intertwining math and crafts; no doubt you'll think of many more.

How to Practice Math While Working on Craft Projects

/ Laying out and cutting patterns is a good way to learn about translations, rotations, and reflections (see #45). Help your children see how to use a piece of cloth most efficiently (with the least waste) and how to lay out the pattern so that stripes, plaids, and other designs match from section to section.

/ You can't be a good knitter if you can't count. Show children how to count rows and stitches as they work.

/ Besides challenging eye-hand coordination, most model kits require good spatial visualization skills. With a few kits behind them, children will find that their ability to predict a finished product from a handful of parts is much improved. Children will look at directions less often as they start to see the relationships among shapes and among parts of a whole.

/ Buy your junior craftspeople their own measuring tapes and demonstrate how to use them. Give them a shoebox full of scrap materials and challenge each child to build something.

/ Making dollhouse furniture is a painless introduction to ratios and proportions (see #48). Have children compare themselves to the dolls for whom they're designing in order to create furniture that is in proportion.

5.

Suggest Practical Reasons
for Math: Your Job

I'm amused by the new trend in cash registers, first seen at chains like McDonald's. Instead of having numbers, the keys on the register have pictures of the items sold. Pressing a picture key brings up the cost of the item instantly. The machine totals the items, as most cash registers do. The cashier must then punch in the amount of money handed over by the customer (the only hands-on involvement of numbers required, for the register then calculates the change to be received). Recognition of coins and bills is just about the only math skill needed.

Although it seems as though technology is eliminating the need for basic skills, Although it seems as though technology is eliminating the need for basic skills, you will find, when you think about it, that you still use math on the job. If you're a contractor, cook, or registered nurse, you need to read instruments of measure. If you're a buyer, shop owner, or manufacturer, you deal with time schedules, costs, and quantities of materials. Your children—the ones who constantly whine, "Why do I need to know this?"—can benefit greatly from a visit to your place of employment to see math in action.

Before inviting your children for a visit, think about the answers to these questions:

1. How do I use math on the job? Do I calculate salaries or costs? Do I measure or weigh? Do I deal with patterns or designs? Do I read graphs, tables, or gauges? What kinds of problems do I solve?

2. Why is it important that I be able to calculate well and quickly on the job?

3. What other "school" skills do I use on the job? Do I read? Do I write? Do I use speaking and listening skills? How?

Answering these questions for yourself will help you focus your children's visit on the way the skills they are just learning affect your job.

As your children visit your workplace, show them step-by-step what you do on a typical day. Demonstrate tools that make your job easier. Try to relate what you do to what your children do:

"You know the calculator you use in school? Look at the fancy one I get to use here!"

"Remember how you had some trouble with bar graphs? Look at the amazing graphs we just got from the marketing department!"

"What I'm doing now is just like solving a word problem. I look for the question that's being asked and decide what I need to do step-by-step to find the solution."

Knowing what you do all day long helps your children understand you better. It also helps them see why their occupation—learning in school—is so important to their futures.

6.

Provide Concrete Manipulatives

Walking into Willow Creek Day Care Center, a visitor is struck at once by an air of controlled pandemonium. Fifteen children are playing half a dozen different games. Three boys are stacking cubes to make a tower. A little girl is winding yarn around pegs on a board. Two children, clearly too young to play checkers, are arranging checkers in rows on a checkerboard. A boy is building something elaborate with coffee stirrers. Several children are rolling out clay in preparation for making "pots." Three girls sit at a table while a boy hands each a teacup for "tea." As the aides circulate and quietly quiz the children about what they are doing, it becomes clear that every hands-on game is really a learning task.

Children's intellectual development is gradual and continuous. No child wakes up one morning able to add and subtract. The Swiss child psychologist Jean Piaget identified four main influences on children's development. Perhaps the most important of these is *experience*.

When Piaget spoke of experience, he meant contact with physical objects. For example, *physical experience* gives children the knowledge that a feather is lighter than a spoon. Out of this physical experience comes *logical-mathematical experience*, in which the child learns a principle by performing actions on objects. By manipulating spoons, for example, a child might learn that a stack of four spoons contains the same number of spoons as a row of four spoons.

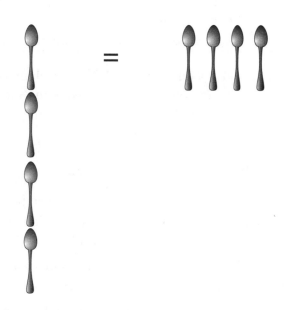

Before any child is ready to perform the simplest addition and subtraction on paper, he or she must have had thousands of concrete experiences with real objects. This doesn't mean that parents have to run out to a store and purchase expensive math toys. The simple toys at Willow Creek Day Care support a variety of concepts.

Toy	Logical-Mathematical Experience
Stacking cubes	Shape, volume, symmetry, number
Yarn and pegs	Shape, perimeter, patterns
Checkers	Number, one-to-one correspondence, patterns
Coffee stirrers	Shape, perimeter, symmetry, patterns
Clay	Shape, volume
Teacups	Number, one-to-one correspondence, volume

Although you cannot speed up your child's development (see #18 for more about the pace of development), you can provide the tools for discovery and help children express their findings. Here are a few manipulative activities to try.

How to Practice Math Using Manipulatives

Suppose your preschooler is banging on pots and pans in the kitchen. Ask, "Which one makes the deepest noise? Which one is the biggest? Which two make noises that are about the same?"

Give an older child three different-colored blocks and ask how many different-colored trains he or she can make.

Have preschoolers sort balls or blocks by color and size.

As your children play in the sandbox, talk to them about what they are making and how they are making it.

Have your children explain the parts and workings of a favorite toy or game.

Challenge a child to mirror your actions and make patterns with checkers on a checkerboard. Ask, "How did you know where to put each checker?"

By asking questions that illuminate what your child is discovering, you help the child make connections, increase observational skills, and build a foundation of knowledge about the world. Children must pass through this experiential stage of development before they can achieve the abstract thinking that is needed in much of mathematics. Does your child count on his or her fingers to add or subtract? It's not a sign of ignorance. By manipulating objects (in this case, fingers), children bridge the gap between the concrete, tangible, real world and the abstract world of numbers. Eventually, your child won't need that concrete affirmation but will be confident enough in that abstract world to manipulate numbers without "seeing" them first. A foundation of experience with real objects will make that transition easier.

7.

Keep a Measurement Diary

Karen and her parents moved recently into a house that was built in 1880. In her new bedroom, Karen discovered something amazing: a series of horizontal notches in the wooden door frame with years scratched next to each one. The lowest notch was labeled 1887; the highest was 1900. Fascinated, Karen realized that a child who slept in this very room had once kept track of his or her growth with a pocket knife. Immediately, Karen and her brothers wanted to do the same thing.

To interest children in mathematics, it helps to move concepts from the abstract to the concrete and to personalize them. An easy way to do this is with a measurement diary.

Children love to see how they have changed over time. Did you make a baby book? This might be a good time to review it. Point out your children's original birth weights and lengths (heights). Then help them weigh and measure themselves now. What's the difference? How much have they grown?

You'll need a scale, a measuring tape, and a straightedge if you want to start keeping records of children's growth. Give each child a small notebook in which to record statistics. Some interesting statistics to keep track of include weight, height, arm length from shoulder to tip of middle finger, neck circumference, waist circumference, and head circumference.

Once a month, encourage a weigh-in and recording of statistics. Have children compare each month to the month before. (For more dramatic changes, do this every three months instead.) At the end of the year, you might help children graph their growth for a visual reminder of the changes they've made.

8.

Have Children Plan Trips

> "The kind of problem I hate," Brian remarks crankily, "is that stupid 'One car takes off from point A going 40 miles an hour, and another starts from point B going 50 miles an hour, and when will they crash, or whatever.' Who cares?"

Some of the problems Brian hates are just brainteasers or training exercises, but there are plenty of real problems involving real travel that can teach children all sorts of skills. Planning a trip entails a number of mathematical concepts—including addition, decimals, division, estimation, measurement, and time.

 Addition. A road map requires you to add many small numbers to determine your total mileage. By adding and then comparing numbers, you can find the shortest route to your planned destination.

Decimals. Your car holds 15 gallons of gas. Gas is $1.32 per gallon. How much does it cost to fill an empty tank? Your odometer reads 13989.7. How much farther will you drive before you hit 14,000 miles? If the nearest exit is 12 miles away, what will your odometer read when you reach the exit?

Division. You go 265 miles before filling up the tank with 15 gallons of gas. How many miles does your car average per gallon? Your trip is approximately 280 miles, and you'll average 50 miles per hour. How long will it take to arrive at your destination?

Estimation. The sign says that your exit is 3 miles away. How soon should you look for the turnoff? You've been traveling for nearly an hour at speeds from 30 to 60 miles per hour. About how far are you from your destination? You need to fill up the car, but you have only $15. About how much gas can you buy?

Measurement. Converting kilometers to miles (or miles to kilometers) may be necessary. You'll certainly need to measure gas, mileage, and time.

| 1 mile | = | 1.61 kilometers |
| 1 kilometer | = | .62 miles |

Time. Are we there yet? No, we'll be there in 45 minutes. How long is that? You can gain a good sense of elapsed time while sitting in the back seat of a car. While planning a trip, you'll need to have a sense of how long it takes to travel a given distance.

You might begin by having kids plan a short trip to a nearby town. Give them a map and help them find a route that makes sense. Just for fun, have them locate an alternative route for the trip home. Show how to measure the mileage and estimate together how long the trip might take at a given average miles per hour. Discuss how much gas that might mean for your particular car, and decide whether you need to fill the tank.

As children show proficiency at simple trip planning, you can involve them in planning vacations, trips to Grandma's, and so on. It's a great way to see math in action.

9.

Use Long Car Trips as Adventures in Math

> You're traveling 3,000 miles in a beat-up station wagon with a dog and three children between the ages of 6 and 12. If you cover 300 miles a day, where will you be when (1) the car overheats? (2) the dog gets carsick? (3) each child needs to use the restroom?

If planning a trip affords ample opportunities to explore math concepts, traveling offers even more. Think of the numbers that have significance on the road: mileposts, odometer readings, gas prices, the distance to the nearest Burger King. . . .

How to Use Long Car Trips to Practice Math

Assign a child to navigate. Depending on each child's age, he or she might read the map and estimate distances to the exit you want, read mileage signs, or alert you to the gas station sign that advertises the best price per gallon.

Play look-out-the-window games. Counting games are easy and fun for children of all ages. Be the first to find 10 red cars or 5 restaurant billboards. Count out-of-state license plates, recreational vehicles, or cars with only one person inside. Challenge children to find license plates that have some of the same numerals as yours or license plates that contain their ages.

Estimate. Have children estimate how far they can see along the road in both directions. Then have them count all the cars they see and project the number of cars along a 5- or 10-mile stretch of road. Alternatively, tell the children when you will stop next—for example, in about 10 minutes. Have them call out when they think the time is up. (This can be really annoying at first, but they will get better at estimating time if they practice.)

Play number games. Have passengers in the car take turns adding strings of one-digit numbers:

> Player 1: "One plus five equals six."
>
> Player 2: "Plus two equals eight."
>
> Player 3: "Plus three equals eleven."
>
> Player 4: "Plus six equals seventeen. . . ."

Alternatively, try a guessing game: "I'm thinking of a number between 1 and 20. It is divisible by 6 and 2, but it is not divisible by 4. It is greater than 7. What is it?" (18)

Play travel-related games. Work as a family to name the states that have four letters in their names, the states that have five letters in their names, and the states with more than ten letters in their names. Figure out how many states border the one you're in. Use a map to determine the shapes of states and countries. Which ones are nearly rectangles? Which are irregular polygons, shapes with straight sides of differing lengths?

Try pencil-and-paper games. Here's a game of strategy: On a pad of paper, draw ten rows of ten dots. Children pass the pad back and forth and take turns connecting two dots horizontally or vertically with a line segment. If a child connects the two dots that finish enclosing a square, the child writes his or her initials in the square. When all dots are connected, the child with the most squares wins. Tic-tac-toe is another strategy game. Problem-solving paper games include the following:

1. Use 1-centimeter graph paper. Draw the rectangle composed of nine one-centimeter squares that has the greatest possible perimeter (9×1). Now draw the rectangle composed of nine squares that has the least possible perimeter (3×3).

2. In this town there are four perfectly straight roads. Where any two roads cross, there is an intersection. No matter how the roads are arranged, there will be no more than six intersections. Try drawing lines representing roads to see for yourself. Now decide what the largest possible number of intersections there will be in a town with six perfectly straight roads ($1 + 2 + 3 + 4 + 5 = \underline{15}$).

3. Divide the following shape into five identically shaped pieces, each of which contains a dot. (The solution is provided at the end of this section.)

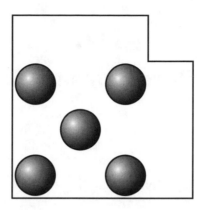

When you simply want the children to be quiet so that you can drive in peace, brainteaser books are a great idea. They come in all types for all ages. Some possibilities are listed here.

Some Useful Brainteaser Books

Author	Title	Difficulty Level
Anno, Mitsumasa	*Anno's Math Games I & II*	Easy
Bodycombe, David	*The Mammoth Book of Brainstorming Puzzles*	Challenging
Burns, Marilyn	*The I Hate Mathematics! Book*	Average
Gardner, Martin	*Perplexing Puzzles and Tantalizing Teasers*	Average
Phillips, Louis	*263 Brain Busters: Just How Smart Are You, Anyway?*	Average

10.

Have Children Design Schedules

You've asked Johnny to clean his room 14 times this week. If it's only Tuesday morning, how many more times can you expect to ask him before the task is actually accomplished?

Children aren't born with a built-in sense of elapsed time. They develop that sense through practice. It's quite typical for young children to believe that summer vacation lasts longer than the school year or that "just five minutes" means something on the order of half an hour. If you are constantly at odds with your children because of their immature senses of time, perhaps it's time for you to help them practice.

One way to help children develop a better sense of time is to encourage them to design schedules of events that are meaningful to them. Here are some ideas.

How to Use Schedules to Practice Math

 Encourage children to design their own TV-watching schedules, based on TV listings and a set number of hours a week you will let them watch.

Discuss household chores and the length of time each should reasonably take. Devise together a chart of weekly chores that divides the workload evenly in the number of hours.

If getting ready for school each day is a struggle, have children draw a timeline showing what needs to be done in the morning and how long it should take. Decide together how to set the alarm clock so that everything gets done with time to spare. Check your timeline against a real-life run-through and adjust your clock setting according to your results.

On a visit to the zoo or museum when you are pressed for time, have children determine which exhibits to see and how long to spend at each one to complete their visit in the time you have allotted.

11.

Set the Table Together

Your good china has mysteriously shrunk by two place settings. You find one bowl being used as a dog dish, and a plate and saucer glued together as part of a science experiment. How many dishes are left unaccounted for?

Many household chores offer opportunities to practice math concepts of one sort or another. The simple act of setting a table presents a variety of possibilities.

How to Use Table Settings to Practice Math

Practice the directional concepts *left, right, over, under, up,* and *down* as you have your youngest children place napkins, plates, and cutlery correctly on the table.

Ask young children to count the people in the family and then count out the correct number of forks, spoons, and knives for a family dinner.

Discuss the relative sizes of plates and saucers and of tablespoons and teaspoons.

Have older children work at making place settings as symmetrical as possible or at making the table as a whole exactly symmetrical. Is it possible?

Discuss ratio and proportion by asking how the number of forks or cups would change if your family doubled in size, tripled in size, grew by half, and so on.

12.

Look for Patterns

The ability to recognize and continue patterns is an important prerequisite to the mastery of mathematics. When mathematicians speak of patterns, they may be referring to visual patterns, or they may mean numerical patterns. Recognizing either kind of pattern requires logical thinking. From a very young age, children can practice this skill.

Finding visual patterns is easy to practice. On a rainy day, have children look for repeating patterns in the house—floor tiles, upholstery patterns, and so on. Discuss the kinds of patterns found, which may include mirror symmetry, horizontal repetition, and radiating patterns. Children should be able to "read" a pattern aloud—for example, "Thick blue stripe, thin red stripe, thick blue stripe, thin red stripe."

How to Practice Looking for Patterns

When your children become fairly expert at finding and describing patterns, hand out art materials and have them design their own patterns. (See #44 for more on visual patterns.)

Numerical patterns require at least an elementary understanding of number theory, so practice in these patterns can probably wait until children are school-age. In first grade, children can start counting by twos, fives, and tens. You can give them simple "adding-on" patterns to continue:

$$1 + 3 = 4 + 3 = 7 + 3 = 10 + 3 = ? \ (\underline{13})$$

Older children can solve pattern brainteasers such as this:

Find the next number: 7, 14, 28, 56, ? ($\underline{112}$)

The children should be able to explain the pattern in words. (Each number is twice the number before.)

By the time they are teenagers, children should be able to solve complex brainteasers and even make up their own for family members to solve:

Find the next number: 1, 6, 21, 66, 201, ? ($\underline{606}$)

(Multiply each number by 3 and add 3.)

If you present numerical patterns as a game, most children will take to them with glee. The practice they get in thinking logically and internalizing number theory makes pattern games invaluable.

13.

Discuss an Allowance

 When you were Tommy's age, you got a quarter a week. By the time your sister was Tommy's age, she got 50 cents a week. Now Tommy has friends who get $5.00 a week. Where will it end?

Before you completely reject the idea of an allowance for your children, consider that children better understand money values when they have their own money to save or spend. When they ask you for money to buy things they want, children gain no sense that there is a reasonable limit to the amount they can spend. Money means more when it is clearly finite.

When your children reach allowance age, sit them down and talk about wise use of money. Have them give specific examples of items they would like to save for and buy. (See #14 for ideas on setting up a savings plan.)

Discuss a reasonable amount for an allowance. Don't be cowed by talk of how much Susie or Derwood gets each week; settle on a figure that makes sense to you.

It's useful to give an allowance that carries with it the expectation of work. Some chores should be mandatory and not rewarded with money, but overtime or extra chores might be compensated. If you want, peg increases to productivity. For example, suggest that if your child's room is spotless for three months, you might consider a raise.

Open a bank account for older children and show them how to deposit and withdraw funds. Read statements together as they arrive. Show your children how money can grow even as it sits in a bank. Teenagers might like to look at ways to make their money grow faster. Have them compare interest rates at local banks and look at alternatives to regular savings accounts such as CDs or money market funds.

14.
Make a Savings Plan

The toy store is advertising an Easter special on Beanie Babies™—two for $5.00 while supplies last. The sale is two weeks away. Lisa has saved $3.50 and gets 50 cents allowance each week. When should she start begging?

Wise children will exploit their parents for the loot to obtain the toy of their dreams. Wise parents will turn the tables on their children, using the kids' desires as an opportunity to teach them the value of a dollar. When children want a particular toy or other treat, encourage them to start a savings plan.

To start such a plan, you first need to know the following information:

1. The cost of the item, including tax

2. The amount of money the child has now

3. The amount of income the child expects

4. Any additional expenses

With this information on hand, you can help children create a timeline that will help them determine how long it might take to be able to buy the desired item.

You have $3.50. The item costs $5.00 plus 7% tax, or $5.35. You receive 50 cents a week.			
Next week: You have $4.00.	In 2 weeks: You have $4.50.	In 3 weeks You have $5.00.	In 4 weeks: You have $5.50.

Have children make a plan and stick to it. If they are desperate to purchase the item in a shorter period of time (in the case of a special sale or limited offer), suggest ways they might earn the money they need in less time. If you think it's helpful, add incentives: If the child sticks to the plan for three weeks, you will provide the remaining money needed; or if the child saves every dime of his or her allowance, you will pay for incidental expenses during a four-week period. Keep in mind that for a small child with a special toy in mind, four weeks can be an awfully long time.

Knowing how to save is one of those so-called "real life" skills that is vitally important to survival as an adult. With a little imagination, you can make savings fun for children. Provide a fascinating place to deposit funds, perhaps a piggy bank shaped like a safe, a grown-up's leather wallet, or a real savings account in a bank. Offer matching funds for long-term savings or show children how interest accrues on money they deposit. An end-of-the-year accounting showing how their savings have grown can be a terrific incentive for children and a source of great pride.

15.

Play Cards

 You've played twenty games of "Old Maid" with your sick eight-year-old, and he has won every hand. What are the odds that you'll win the next game?

Card games are a wonderful way to pass the time when children are ill, snowed in, or simply bored. Most card games involve several number-related skills as well as problem-solving strategies, logical thinking, and spatial visualization. Here are a few simple children's games and the skills they reinforce.

Some Simple Card Games

Concentration

Skills: number recognition, spatial visualization

Rules: Shuffle cards and lay them randomly face down on the table or floor. The object is to collect pairs of cards with the same number or picture. Players take turns turning up two cards. If the cards match, the player keeps them and takes another turn. If the cards do not match, the player returns them face down. The winner is the player with the most pairs at the end.

Go Fish

Skills: number recognition, strategy

Rules: Deal a hand to each player and a spare hand face down until all the cards are dealt. Each player will try to get rid of all his or her cards. Players sort their cards in their hands into groups with the same number or picture. Then one player asks another for a particular card to match one he or she already has; for example, if the player already holds the 3 of spades, that player might ask for the 3 of clubs. If the other player does not have that card, the response is "Go fish." The first player must then take a card from the face-down pile. If the second player does have the card, that player must hand it over, and the first player may ask again. When four cards in a suit are collected, they may be placed face down in a pile. Play ends when one player gets rid of all cards.

My Ship Sails

Skills: counting, strategy

Rules: Deal seven cards to each of four to seven players. Discard the other cards. Players sort their hands into suits. Based on their sorting, they determine which suit they will try to collect. Each player discards one unwanted card to the player on the right. Play continues in this way until the winner collects seven cards in the same suit. That player cries "My ship sails!"

Sequence

Skill: number sequence

Rules: Deal a hand to each player until all cards are dealt. The first player places his or her lowest card of any suit face up in the center. The player with the next card in sequence and in the same suit places it face up on that card. Play continues until the ace in that suit is played; the player who played that card may start the next sequence. The first player to get rid of all cards wins.

War

Skills: number value, comparing numbers

Rules: Deal all the cards to two players. Players place their cards face down in a pile without looking at them. Both players turn over their top card. The player with the higher card wins both cards and places them in the bottom of his or her pile. If two cards are turned up that have the same value, it's war: Each player puts one card face down on top of that first card in a separate pile and then turns the next card face up. The higher card wins all six cards. The winner is the player who ends up with all the cards.

16.

Encourage Sports Connections

Player A batted .350 for half the season. After he was injured, he came back and played in the play-offs, but he batted only .175. When can he expect to be traded?

My brother learned all the statistics he knows from baseball cards. I know several men who can't add a column of figures but can give you the spread on every NFL game from the season opener to the Super Bowl. Another close friend couldn't tell you what a flowchart is for but can explain the significance of every NCAA team's placement in the flowchart that leads to the Final Four.

Many of these people might claim to dislike math. They don't see their interest in sports trivia as having anything to do with math. They are wrong.

Pick a sport. Track and field is all about measurements: heights, times, and distances. Football is yards gained and lost and scores that require adding ones, twos, threes, and sixes. Understanding golf means understanding negative numbers. Baseball is loaded with statistics: earned run averages, runs batted in, and batting averages. Tracking a single baseball player's season is an adventure in mathematics.

If you have children who already show an interest in sports, by all means encourage them. (You don't have to rub it in—"You're using math, honey!") Help them collect sports cards (throw out that awful gum) and take an interest in their interests. Discuss why Player A is better than Player B, or why Team X is expected to walk all over Team Y. You may be surprised to learn that your child can explain the meaning of those mysterious batting averages better than you can.*

Open any sports almanac (my favorite is the one published by *Information Please*). Every page is loaded with numbers: win-loss ratios, scores, field goal percentages, stadium capacities, relay times, power play conversions, and salary caps. If your children spend time browsing in the almanac, reading the back of their sports cards, or just checking scores in the daily newspaper, they are using math voluntarily, effortlessly, and with a solid conceptual understanding they may rarely demonstrate at school.

---

*Note: In its simplest form, a batting average is the number of hits divided by the number of times at bat, expressed as a decimal to the nearest thousandth. To achieve a batting average of .350, you could be at bat 100 times and hit 35, or you could be at bat 20 times and hit 7, and so on. Every game in which a player is at bat affects and alters his batting average, yet true baseball fans are able to quote a given player's average at the drop of a hat.

17.

Evaluate Statistics

Today's newspaper cites a study of Americans and their causes of death. Apparently, the greatest number of deaths due to heart disease occur in the Southeast. Why is this statistic potentially misleading? (Hint: Who moves to Florida, and why?)

If you gulp down what the media feed you undigested, you will have a hard time getting out of bed in the morning. Judging by the tabloid news, you should regularly find yourself beating your latchkey child while an out-of-control asteroid threatens your crime-ridden town and its mostly unemployed citizens.

One thing that math literacy gives us is the ability to sift data and decide what they mean for ourselves. Understanding statistics can make us more comfortable with the vast amounts of data that bombard us daily. When I went to school, many children were afraid of the atom bomb. Nowadays, children might fear random gunshots through the school window, strange men kidnapping them on the playground, or aliens whisking them away to distant planets. You do your children a real service if you start evaluating statistical data with them regularly.

A book published in 1954 is still my favorite reference tool for people who want to know how to digest statistics with the proper grain of salt. *How to Lie with Statistics*, by Darrell Huff (W. W. Norton & Company), teaches you how advertisers, sociologists, and other statisticians use biased samples, truncated graphs, and irrelevant figures to prove anything they desire. It's a lot of fun, and your older kids will enjoy it, too.

How to Evaluate Statistics

Have children sift through the newspaper to find examples of statistics. These might be in an article about a science experiment, a census, election results, or any number of other topics. Discuss these questions:

1. What sample was used? Was it large or small? (For example, an exit poll that interviews six people at one polling place is probably not very significant.)

2. What question was being asked? Do the results really answer the question?

3. Are the conclusions the scientists, pollsters, or journalists drew from the statistics logical?

Look at graphs with your children. Newsmagazines and *USA Today* are good sources. Do line and bar graphs be at zero? If not, they are designed to deceive you. Pictographs are often extremely misleading, as this example shows:

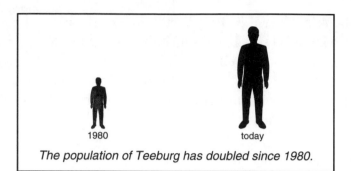

The population of Teeburg has doubled since 1980.

The pictograph for "today" is twice as tall as the one for 1980, but it is also twice as wide, giving the impression of a far greater (quadruple rather than double) growth than what occurred in reality.

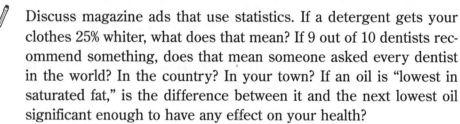 Discuss magazine ads that use statistics. If a detergent gets your clothes 25% whiter, what does that mean? If 9 out of 10 dentists recommend something, does that mean someone asked every dentist in the world? In the country? In your town? If an oil is "lowest in saturated fat," is the difference between it and the next lowest oil significant enough to have any effect on your health?

Solution to Game on Page 27

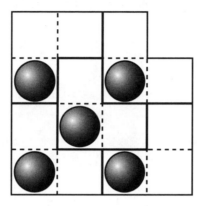

SECTION 2

Modify
Children's Behavior

18.

Make Sure Your Child is Ready for Math Concepts

Gabriel's mother made lemonade and poured Gabriel and his sister Jennifer each a glass. Gabriel had a fit because Jennifer got a tall glass, and he got one that was short and squat. Even when his mother showed him that both glasses held the same 8 ounces, he insisted on having the tall glass, claiming it held more.

The Swiss psychologist Jean Piaget was among the first to explore the fact that children pass through discrete stages of learning. They may reach the steps at different ages, but every child goes through the same steps in the same order.

In mathematics, the relevant learning steps have to do with what is called *conservation*. Piaget refers to several forms of conservation, including conservation of number, of continuous quantity, and of substance.

Conservation of number has to do with the ability to recognize one-to-one correspondence. Give your child a set of four objects and a box of other objects. Ask him or her to construct a set with the same number of objects as your set. The child who does not yet count may still be able to do this task by putting out one object for each one in your set. Very young children, however, will fail completely.

If you give many six-year-olds objects configured as in the following drawing, they will understand that each group has the same number of objects, even though they are organized differently. Many four-year-olds, however, will accept that the A groups contain the same number but think that the B groups do not.

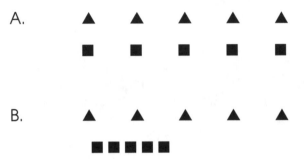

A child who can conserve number can build two sets equivalent in number and can *conserve* the equivalence even when the sets are rearranged. A child who has not reached this stage cannot be expected to add or subtract with any authority or even to understand that a numeral stands for a certain number or value. That is why you may find your kindergarten or first-grade child practicing drawing lines to match objects in workbook activities. You may think, What does this have to do with math? In fact, it has everything to do with being *ready* for math.

Conservation of continuous quantity involves the ability to understand that a quantity does not change even after a variety of manipulations. To test this, you might pour 6 ounces of juice into two 8-ounce glasses of the same shape. Your child might agree that the glasses hold the same amount. Then pour the contents of one glass into a third, differently shaped glass. Ask your child whether the two glasses that are filled hold the same amount. A child who can conserve continuous quantity will understand that the amount of juice has not changed just because the shape of the container makes it appear different.

Conservation of substance is similar but involves solid objects. Traditionally, a ball of clay is split into two equal balls, and the child is asked whether they are the same size. Then one of the balls is rolled into a snake, and the same question is asked. A child who can conserve substance knows that the amount of clay does not change simply because the shape changes.

Piaget found that all children begin by being unable to conserve. They then progress through a time of trial and error until they are able to conserve. For example, in the case of conservation of continuous quantity, a preschooler may recognize that the two glasses of the same size and shape hold the same amount. A kindergartner may say that the liquid in a wider or taller glass is greater. A first or second grader will probably recognize that the amount of liquid does not change, and will be able to give reasons for this conclusion.

It's clear that to progress through these stages with ease, children need a variety of experiences with manipulating objects (see #6). It is also clear that forcing children to do math when they are not ready is a fruitless task. Some children can conserve numbers when they are three. Others can't do it until they are six or seven. It's easy enough to find out where your child stands— simply try the experiments just described. Unfortunately, it's quite impossible to teach conservation through drill or lecture; it is one of those magical connections children must make on their own. Until they do, provide hands-on experiences and be patient.

THERE ARE THREE KINDS OF PEOPLE:
THOSE WHO CAN COUNT
AND THOSE WHO CAN'T

91A 5351

19.

Promote Understanding Over Memorization

Many years ago I taught a first grader who could read *Hop on Pop* cover to cover without stumbling once. Astonishingly, he could not tell me what any word in the book meant; he spoke only Japanese. He had learned English phonics very well and had memorized letter-sound combinations, but he hadn't a clue what he was reading.

There is no question that memorization is important to math literacy. Just as children must internalize English grammar and learn letter-sound combinations by heart, so must they internalize the grammar of mathematics. They do this by memorizing times tables and adding one-digit numbers in all directions until they can do it in their sleep. It's dull, but it's vital. However, memorization alone doesn't do the trick. Would you want a medical student to operate on you simply because he or she could recite the names of all your nerves and muscles?

It's very possible for children to know their times tables but not be able to explain what multiplication is or when you should use it. It's equally possible for children to recite, "Two plus three is five, three plus two is five," but not be able to apply this commutative property when making change from a five-dollar bill. (See #25 for more on the commutative property.)

Textbooks try to get at this need for application by ending every set of calculations with a few word problems. Children don't necessarily see the connection, though. You can help your child explore the meaning behind pages of calculations by asking a few illuminating questions about their homework. The following questions are simply examples:

- **For a page on adding:** "How would you check those? Why does that work?" (By subtracting—because in addition you're putting sets together, and in subtracting you're taking them apart again.)

- **For a page on adding and subtracting money:** "Which of those is less than a dollar? If those were purchases, could you pay for them all with a hundred-dollar bill?"

- **For a page on subtracting four-digit numbers:** "When might you have to subtract such big numbers?" (For example, to compare long distances or large amounts.)

- **For a page on multiplying by 2:** "Why aren't any of your answers odd numbers?" (Only even numbers have 2 as a factor.)

- **For a page on dividing by 7:** "What does it mean that 28 divided by 7 equals 4?" (It means you can fit 4 groups of 7 in 28.)

It's helpful to ask questions such as *Why? What does this mean?* and *How does this work?* At times, you may not know the answer yourself. Don't worry. Working together, you and your children should be able to come up with a solution that makes sense. At the very least, children may come away with a good question to pose at school the next day.

Another way to explore the meaning of mathematics is to provide some manipulatives such as coins or buttons and have children demonstrate one of their calculations for you.

$$28 \div 7 = 4$$

⊗ ⊗ ⊗ ⊗ ⊗ ⊗ ⊗
⊗ ⊗ ⊗ ⊗ ⊗ ⊗ ⊗
⊗ ⊗ ⊗ ⊗ ⊗ ⊗ ⊗
⊗ ⊗ ⊗ ⊗ ⊗ ⊗ ⊗

28 buttons divided into groups of 7 makes 4 rows of 7.

This activity is especially useful if your child learns best by seeing or manipulating objects, as many children do.

Too many children excel at memorization and stumble through math classes, getting good grades without ever really "getting it." Your children can't really love math unless they do "get it," unless they grasp the meaning that underlies their neat columns of figures.

20.

Help Eradicate Math Myths

"It's not surprising that Rachel is rotten at math," her mother confided. "I was always terrible at it."

"Oh, really?" I carelessly answered. "Is it genetic?"

"Maybe it is," she replied thoughtfully. "After all, those Chinese kids are so good at it, aren't they?"

To eradicate math myths in your children, you must first recognize and quash them in your own point of view. Once you've done that, you can answer swiftly when your children use math myths to excuse their poor performance.

Some people are just good at math.

Perhaps the number-one myth standing in the way of student success is the one that says you need a certain mind-set or innate ability to be good at math. In their book *The Learning Gap,* authors Harold Stevenson and James Stigler explore the differences among Chinese, Japanese, and American schools. They compare the American emphasis on ability to the Asian emphasis on effort.

Asians tend to believe that anyone can learn with the proper effort. Americans, who dote on such things as IQ tests and tracking, prefer to think that some people have a natural ability to learn certain subjects and others do not. It's a strange attitude for a supposedly democratic country to take, but it's quite deeply felt. Stevenson and Stigler use the example of art: An American who can't create a credible representation of a flower might say, "I'm no good at drawing," whereas a Japanese or Chinese visitor might reply, "It's too bad no one taught you to draw."

It's okay to be bad at math.

"Only in mathematics," says the National Research Council's 1989 report on the future of math education, "is poor school performance socially acceptable." Many parents rush to accept a grade in math that they would deplore if it showed up on a penmanship report. This goes back to the assumption of native ability described above. Can the fact that 50 percent of Japanese students match the math performance of our top 5 percent really mean that they're somehow genetically better in math? Could it be that our bad attitude toward math makes it easy for our children to fail?

If a math problem is solvable, it can be solved quickly.

Stevenson and Stigler again contrast American students with Asian students. In a computation test featuring timed problems, Americans attempted the most problems and solved the fewest. When the solution did not present itself quickly, the Americans skipped to the next problem. The Asian students, on the other hand, plodded methodically through until they solved the few problems they started. The fact is, of course, that not all problems are solved quickly; the most interesting problems require effort and time.

Computers and calculators mean math is obsolete.

Thanks to computers, mathematics is even more vital and useful than it was in the past. Computers use mathematical models to predict earthquakes, design museums, and analyze election returns. We have the results thrown at us daily in newspaper and television reports. The less we know about math, the more these lightning-quick calculations and analyses are likely to confound us. If our math skills are limited to basic arithmetic, however, our calculators might as well take over for us right now (see #31).

Math is just a rigid set of rules and a lot of arithmetic.

In *Everybody Counts: A Report to the Nation on the Future of Mathematics Education,* the National Research Council calls for math education that teaches mathematical modes of thought. If these modes are taught correctly, the study claims, they will lead to a "capacity of mind that enables one to read critically, to identify fallacies, to detect bias, to assess risk, and to suggest alternatives." The importance of math, in other words, is what it helps us do. Rules and arithmetic are just the path to the goal.

21.

Let Children Take an Interest and Run with It

Rebecca's favorite game is to grab a handful of coins from her father's pocket and stack them by color and size. Her older brother Jeb is into big cats. He likes to draw cougars, tigers, jaguars, and ocelots and label them with statistics about their size and range. Jeb's friend Carl couldn't care less about animals, but he loves cars of all kinds, the faster the better.

"Inquiry-based learning" is a type of instruction in which children are encouraged to take a particular interest of their own and run with it as far as they want to go. What can be chaotic in a classroom of 20-plus children can be simple and fun at home. In inquiry-based learning, all learning stems from the child's own questions about his or her world. It's a natural way of learning that parallels the way your child learned in infancy about the world.

All children are curious about their world. Our tendency, as adults with too much to do and too little time to do it, is to answer their questions and leave it at that. How much better it is to help them discover the answers and see how far their curiosity might take them!

Rebecca is into coins, mostly because they're pretty and fun to stack. Eventually, she's bound to wonder why they come in different sizes. At that point, you can talk about values of coins. She already can sort them; pretty soon she'll be able to find the value of each stack by counting by ones, fives, and tens.

Jeb likes big cats; they're fierce and strong and a little scary. He's willing to do the research to find out their relative sizes and ranges. Make sure you provide books that help him find out even more. Maybe he'll discover that his big drawing of an ocelot is not in proportion to his smaller drawing of a cougar. He might then move toward making proportional drawings based on relative size. You can help by showing him how to use graph paper to draw in proportion, assigning a particular measurement to each square.

Carl's interest in cars could go in many different directions. Perhaps he'll keep records of race cars and their statistics. He might like to use measuring tools to design and build his own soapbox racer.

There's no point to imposing a topic on children who are already open to the world and what it has to offer—kids get enough of that ready-made stuff at school. Let your children show you where to begin. Support their self-education by supplying books and materials that help them discover more about their current passion. Then sit back, relax, and let learning happen.

22.

Have Children Explain Their Strategies

Whitney did well with addition of one-digit numbers, but she seems at a loss adding two-digit numbers. Sam can finish a page of multiplication sentences in no time, yet still manage to get every single word problem on the page wrong. What's going on?

It's a good idea every once in a while to take children's homework assignments and talk through how they got their answers. If you want your children to understand mathematics instead of simply doing it by rote, they must learn to explain their strategies.

Very young children have trouble explaining things step-by-step, so you may need to model an explanation for them. Here are two examples:

Whitney's homework:

$$
\begin{array}{r}
21 \\
+ \ 49 \\
\hline
\end{array}
$$

"I'm adding 21 and 49. I remember that I always have to start with the ones column. 1 + 9 equals 10, so I know already that I'm going to have to carry. I write the zero and carry the 1 ten over to the tens column. I add that 1 to the 2 and 4 already there, for a total of 7 tens. So the answer is 70."

Sam's homework:

Mr. Green packed 12 eggs each into 5 cartons. How many eggs did he pack?

"I can tell that my answer will be a total number of eggs. Twelve eggs are in each carton, and there are 5 cartons. Because the same number of eggs is in each one, I can multiply. 12×5 is the same as 6×10, so the answer is 60."

Your children's examples may not be as sophisticated as yours. For example, Sam might not see right away the correlation between 12×5 and 6×10. However, just being able to put their actions into words is a big step toward understanding what they are doing and why.

23.

Analyze Errors Together

Whitney and Jane are in the same class, and they often do their homework together. They are both having trouble adding two-digit numbers. Sam and his friend Anya are equally troubled by word problems involving simple multiplication. Whitney and Jane are getting similar grades in math, as are Sam and Anya, but their errors are very different.

Sometimes, children's mistakes in math follow an obvious pattern. If you can discover that pattern through analysis of their errors, you can usually nip the problem in the bud.

Look at these examples from the friends' homework assignments.

Whitney's homework: 21   Jane's homework: 21
                    + 49   + 49
                    ————   ————
                      60   610

Whitney began correctly. She added 1 + 9, got 10, and wrote down the zero. Then she forgot to regroup, or carry the 1 ten, so she simply added 2 + 4, got 6, and wrote her answer, 60.

Jane added 1 + 9, got 10, and wrote 10. Then she added the numbers in the tens column. Both girls' answers were marked wrong, but their problems are quite different.

Whitney understands the principle behind regrouping; she just forgets at times to do it. She could benefit from immediately writing in the tens column the ten to be carried and then adding:

$$\begin{array}{r} 1 \\ 21 \\ + \ 49 \\ \hline 70 \end{array}$$

Jane doesn't understand carrying or regrouping at all. She simply adds both columns as though she were adding ones. Not only that, but she doesn't recognize that her answer has three places, meaning that its value is in the hundreds. She needs remedial work with place value to help her comprehend the difference between ones and tens and tens and hundreds.

Sam's homework:	Mr. Green packed 12 eggs each into 5 cartons. How many eggs did he pack?
	$12 + 5 = \underline{17}$
Anya's homework:	Mr. Green packed 12 eggs each into 5 cartons. How many eggs did he pack?
	$5 \times 12 = \underline{15}$

Sam doesn't know what operation to use to solve the problem (see #34). He knows what the question is and that it's a question of how many in all, but that makes him think of addition rather than multiplication.

Anya, however, realizes that multiplication is called for, but fails to multiply correctly. Because she is multiplying in her head, she accidentally multiplies 5×1 first and writes the answer in the ones column. Then she multiplies 5×2, and, confused, writes the 1 in the tens column. For the time being, Anya should probably set up her numbers vertically so that she can see the columns:

$$
\begin{array}{r}
\overset{1}{1}2 \\
\times\ 5 \\
\hline
60
\end{array}
$$

Once you discover what your child's problem is, you can begin to remediate. A good teacher will compare children's answers and try to analyze their errors, but few teachers have the time to do this for every new concept. Here are some typical errors in children's computation and problem solving:

- Failing to use zero as a placeholder (writing 91 instead of 901)
- Placing regrouped digits in the wrong column
- Choosing the wrong operation
- Aligning digits incorrectly
- Confusing or misreading plus, minus, times, or division signs
- Working too quickly and making careless mistakes
- Failing to recognize reasonable answers (see #43)
- Completing only part of a problem
- Failing to do operations in parentheses first
- Adding the remainder to the quotient
- Using the wrong information to solve a problem

24.

Explore Creative Paths to a Solution

> In geometry class my proofs of geometric principles always wound up having many more steps than the elegant proofs my teacher printed on the board. Of course, it's always neater to have fewer steps, but my answers were correct, too. Sadly, my teacher never mentioned that.

There is no right way to solve a problem. There may be one correct solution, and there may be one path to the solution that is easiest and quickest, but in most cases, there are many possible paths to that solution. Instead of feeling that their processes don't measure up to those in the teacher's editions of their math texts, children need some freedom to experiment with their own paths.

Suppose you were given this problem:

Juan starts work at 8:30 each morning, Monday through Friday. He works until 4:30 Monday through Wednesday and until 3:30 Thursday and Friday. He makes $10/hour. How much does he make in a week?

You might determine the hours Juan works by thinking:

8:30 to 4:30 = 8 hours a day × 3 days a week = 24 hours

8:30 to 3:30 = 7 hours a day × 2 days a week = 14 hours

24 hours + 14 hours = 38 hours

38 hours × $10/hour = $380/week

However, there's nothing wrong with determining how much Juan makes each day and then adding all five figures:

$80 + $80 + $80 + $70 + $70 = $380/week

It may take a little longer and be somewhat less elegant, but you get the same answer in the long run, so who cares?

It's in the best interest of children to use the fastest possible system when they're taking a timed test or working on a huge assignment. Elegance is less important than understanding, though, and understanding often emerges only after much trial and error and many creative approaches to a problem.

How to Explore Creative Paths to a Solution

1. Select multistep problems from your child's textbook.

2. Work the problems as a family, with each person using a path of his or her choice.

3. Talk about the solution and the steps you used to reach it. Did everyone use the same steps?

4. Decide whether there are other ways to get the same answer. Send everyone back to the drawing board to find a path other than the original one he or she chose. Discuss the possibilities. Which path is shortest and fastest?

25.

Try to Prove It

Lenora trotted triumphantly back from the playground, having crushed an opponent in a game of logic.

"Yvette said she hated me infinity times one, and I said I hated her infinity PLUS one, so I win. 'Cause infinity times one might sound like more, but infinity times one is just infinity, and infinity plus one is one MORE than infinity!"

Mathematical proofs are often taught as a discrete skill, tied specifically to Euclidean geometry. That's a shame. Proofs are very useful in helping children understand the logic of mathematics.

In a typical example, you might be asked to prove that when these two sets of parallel lines intersect, angle x has the same measure as angle y.

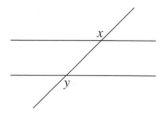

To prove that, you'd need to know a bunch of facts about parallel lines, supplementary angles, parallel lines cut by a transversal, alternate interior angles, and corresponding angles. In other words, to prove that something's true in math, you base your proof on other things that are known to be true. Those known and accepted truths are called *axioms* or *postulates*, and the type of proof is an example of *deductive* reasoning. All true mathematical proofs are deductive.

Another kind of proof is known as an *induction*. You might begin with a theorem, such as "Double any whole number equals an even number." You prove this for the smallest possible value and then prove that if it is true for any value, it is true for the next greater value.

The "proofs" you can do with young children tend to have less to do with logic and more to do with hands-on experimentation or guess-and-test problem solving. Either they are inductive, or they involve reasoning by analogy. You might, for example, try having your children "prove" some of the properties of numbers by using checkers to test each one or by plugging in numbers until they are satisfied that the properties work in "all" cases.

- **Commutative property of addition:** The order in which numbers are added does not affect the sum. $a + b = b + a$

- **Commutative property of multiplication:** The order in which numbers are multiplied does not affect the product. $a \times b = b \times a$

- **Associative property of addition:** The grouping of addends does not affect the sum. $(a + b) + c = a + (b + c)$

- **Associative property of multiplication:** The grouping of factors does not affect the product. $(a \times b) \times c = a \times (b \times c)$

- **Identity property of addition:** Any number plus zero equals that number. $a + 0 = a$

- **Identity property of multiplication:** Any number times one equals that number. $a \times 1 = a$

Other features of whole numbers your children might like to "prove" include these:

- An even number plus 1 equals an odd number.

- An even number times an even number equals an even number.

- An odd number times an odd number equals an even number.

- Any number times 9 has digits whose sum is a multiple of 9.

Once children have tested such statements to their satisfaction, they might use them to invent and prove theorems of their own. For example, knowing that an even number times an even number equals an even number, you could prove that 500 times any multiple of 2 would be an even number. Knowing that any number times 9 has digits that add up to a multiple of 9, you might prove that any number with digits that add up to a multiple of 9, say 333, is divisible by 9. Playing around with numbers in this way helps children internalize the rules of mathematics painlessly, and many children get a kick out of discovering for themselves our number system's built-in logic.

Modify
Your Own Behavior

26.

Put Up a Fearless Front

When I was in college, a friend of my parents asked me whether I was taking any math courses.

"Oh, no," I replied airily. "I was always awful at math."

"What are you talking about?" asked my mother. "Your grades were good, and you even took part in a statewide math contest when you were in junior high."

I was honestly surprised. Based on my own insecurity about my math skills, I had completely rewritten my own history.

What is math anxiety, anyway? Why don't we talk about reading anxiety or social studies anxiety?

Certainly some people are anxious about their own abilities to do math, and rightly so, in many cases. Nevertheless, we all too often let ourselves off the hook by claiming math anxiety instead of facing our fears and dealing with our ignorance. The concept of math anxiety has made it chic to be bad at math. Worse, the attitude that math is scary and difficult produces parents who expect their children to fail.

Do your children a great favor: Even if you suffer from your own math anxiety, don't let it show. Comments such as "Everyone has trouble with math" or "Fractions never made sense to me" just tell your children that they are right to feel fear.

Think about it. What are you afraid of? Your children's math courses aren't using many new, radical approaches that you won't recognize from your own education. If you're genuinely concerned that you won't be able to help with their homework, try looking at their math textbooks while they're asleep or out playing. You may be pleasantly surprised as the concepts come flooding back into your head: measuring perimeter, adding two-digit numbers, rounding. . . . The required skills are not too different from what you use at home or on the job as you work on projects or balance your checkbook.

Suppose your child comes to you with a problem that stumps both of you. It's not the end of the world! Try various techniques to solve it, but if you can't do it, admit that you're stumped. Ask your child to pay attention in class when the problem is discussed and tell you how to solve it once he or she comes home. Most children enjoy playing the part of teacher, and explaining the solution to you helps to reinforce it in your child's mind. It's a great learning tool, and it's far healthier than giving up and blaming your failure on math anxiety.

27.

Take Delight in the Logic of Numbers and Let that Delight Show

> Our seven-month-old daughter is fascinated by objects. She pulls the base off her bottle and holds it over her head, turning it this way and that and admiring it, often cooing or wailing a song in its honor. She seems amazed that it remains the same object whether it's upside down or right side up, and some of her amazement has rubbed off on me. I find myself putting three blocks in a row and then stacking them in a tower, all the while muttering, "Look! It's one, two, three blocks!" I like to pretend that I'm teaching her readiness concepts, but in truth I'm relearning what it's like to discover the world.

Young children spend the greater portion of their waking hours making discoveries about the concrete world. We now know that the more opportunities they have to manipulate a variety of objects in their first three years, the more connections they establish in their brains.

We adults take so much about mathematics for granted. For example, we rarely take the time to wonder why our number system is based on 10. My daughter could tell you: She spends countless hours with her hands in front of her eyes, opening her fists and closing them, seemingly counting her fingers one by one. Sometimes she faces the palms inward, and sometimes she faces them outward. "It's still 10," my husband tells her. And it still is. Isn't that amazing?

You can help your children build on their natural interest in numbers and patterns and at the same time protect them from the numbness and anxiety that school often produces in young students of math. The younger they are when you start, the better.

The first step is to put yourself in your child's shoes and recall what it's like to make discoveries. The second step is to revel in your child's own discoveries. Wow! Two plus two is always four, whether you're adding apples or oranges, whether they're lined up or in a circle, and so on. Gee! A cube is a cube is a cube, whether it's a big yellow one or a tiny red one. Wait a minute! Whether you cut that sandwich in half horizontally or diagonally, we both still get the same amount.

Your enthusiasm for the logic, symmetry, and elegance of mathematics will impress your children. They will bring you their discoveries just for the joy of hearing your excited response. You'll both benefit: They will gain a lifelong appreciation for the wonders of numbers and patterns, and you will recapture some of your childhood zeal for the way the world works.

28.

Monitor Your Attitude for Sexism

In 1992, Mattel, Inc., came out with a new talking Barbie®. Instead of attaining the instant popularity of nearly all other Barbie products, this one produced a firestorm of criticism. Why? Programmed into the anatomically eccentric girl doll was the phrase "Math class is tough." Mattel had to reprogram the dolls.

Much has been made of the presumed "gender gap" in mathematics. A widely quoted 1980 study by Benbow and Stanley claimed that females had less math aptitude genetically than males. The researchers based their supposition on the fact that boys generally do better on standardized tests of mathematical skills.

More recent analyses challenge this finding. Studies cited in the 1992 AAUW Report *How Schools Shortchange Girls* indicate that gender differences are declining and that in classroom work (as opposed to test scores), girls' math grades are equal to or better than boys'.

Despite these analyses, girls rarely take higher math courses, and they are far more likely than boys to think that they're bad at math. This is an impression that gets worse with age. An ETS study called *The Mathematics Report Card* found that 64 percent of third-grade girls think they're good at math, compared to 66 percent of third-grade boys. By high school only 48 percent of girls think they're good at math, compared to 60 percent of boys. This correlates fairly well with ETS's *Trends in Academic Progress*, which reported that in 1990, 9-year-old boys and girls performed nearly equally well on math proficiency tests, but by the age of 17, boys were more proficient. A major study by Fennema and Sherman points to a decline in girls' math confidence around middle school. Surprisingly, the drop in confidence seems to precede the drop in achievement.

Where the gender difference shows up most clearly is in math courses taken and career plans made. Many more boys than girls sign up for calculus in high school, and the few girls who do take calculus rarely plan to go into engineering or other higher-math careers.

It's pretty clear that math anxiety in girls is related to the fallacious message that girls are innately inferior in math. In truth, however, gender differences in mathematics have more to do with acquired skills than with any genetic difference.

Think about the way you play with your children. Often, parents push block building and tool using on boys while leaving dramatizing and language-related games for girls. You've seen that manipulation of objects has a lot to do with children's abilities to grasp math concepts. It's possible that boys' early play better prepares them for higher mathematics.

How to Counteract the Gender Gap in Math

✎ Encourage *all* children to play with blocks and other manipulatives.

✎ Work on building and crafts projects with boys *and* girls. (See #3 and #4.)

Point out women you know or see who use math on the job, from bank tellers and cashiers to brokers and physicists.

Watch adolescent girls for a decline in self-confidence that could lead to poor achievement. Give them extra help and reassurance.

Listen to your words: Do you somehow imply that girls don't need math? Aren't good at math? Can get by without math?

Be aware that you are battling many forces for your daughters' math education. Teachers and guidance counselors are not always as attuned to sexism as you are. Be alert to situations where boys and girls are treated differently in the classroom. Make sure your children's teachers know how you feel—that math is a vital part of *any* child's education. (See #29 for more on dealing with teachers.)

29.

Work with Your Child's Teacher

When Lily started first grade, her mother was busy with two toddlers at home and had little time to pay attention to Lily's schooling. She made sure to read Lily a bedtime story, and she asked her whether her homework was done, but that was all she could manage. It came as a shock, therefore, when Lily's first report card indicated that Lily was foundering in math. Her mother hadn't realized that first graders did much more than count and add to 10.

There is a high correlation between success in school and parental involvement in schooling. For your children to do as well as they possibly can, you must recognize your important role in the learning your child does at school as well as at home.

What do you know about your school's math curriculum? Does it focus on hands-on manipulations of objects? Is there a lot of seat work involving workbook pages, or are children up and about, exploring the living, breathing side of mathematics?

The National Research Council's 1989 study *Everybody Counts* claims that fewer than 10 percent of elementary teachers meet current professional standards for teaching mathematics. That's a shocking statistic. It indicates that

the odds are pretty good that your children's teachers are undertrained and unprepared to teach even rudimentary math skills.

You need to get involved without raising doubts in your children's minds about how they're being taught. You don't want to send the wrong message, but you must be sure they are getting the best math education they can.

Start a relationship with your children's teachers that lets you communicate freely. Find out what materials they use to teach math. If you can, visit the school to see how teachers work with children. Do they consistently call on boys rather than girls? Is there an obvious expectation that some children will be able to do math and others will not? Beyond the students' hearing, politely raise your concerns with the individual teachers.

If your children are doing poorly in math, you need to know about it. Teachers should be able to talk over your children's problems without feeling defensive. You should be able to stay calm when the problems are outlined and suggest or listen to ideas for supplemental help. You want to work as a team with your children's teachers, not as opponents. Remember the goal: to foster in your children math aptitude, math confidence, and a love of math. You and your children's teachers should share that goal.

Lily's story had a happy ending. Her mother took part in a parent-teacher conference, and now she has a much better idea of the first-grade curriculum. She asked the teacher to keep her apprised of what skills are being taught when, and he does so with a written note every few weeks. Now Lily and her mother spend a few minutes before bedtime previewing new skills and reviewing homework. Lily can tell that her mother values math, and her mother now knows that Lily's teacher values Lily's learning.

30.

Be Aware of How Tracking Affects Your Child

David spent the first part of his senior year in high school doing what most of his friends were doing—applying to colleges. He had dreams of being a veterinarian. Much to David's dismay, however, it turned out that he didn't have half the math credits he needed to matriculate at either of the top two colleges of his choice. Several colleges would allow him to enroll, but he would have to waste time and money taking remedial math during his freshman year just to be allowed to take the courses he wanted.

P arents of young children rarely concern themselves with tracking. They should. Although tracking often doesn't kick in for real until middle school, the seeds for it are sown in the primary grades.

In many places today, tracking is subtler than it was 20 years ago, when a student was relegated to the "academic" track or the "vocational" track with no hope of crossing over. The idea was simple: When they got out of high school, academic-track students would go to college. Vocational-track students would get jobs. Vocational-track students, therefore, took "business math," if they took any math at all.

It would be nice to think that all tracking is based strictly on grades or test scores. Unfortunately, as they steer students along, well-meaning but biased and uninformed teachers and guidance counselors often apply several subjective criteria.

Tracking is often classist. A child may be placed in vocational training simply because of his or her background or family history. Tracking is often racist, and when it comes to math, tracking is often sexist.

Very early on, children may be relegated to no-math or low-level math tracks. As with automated rides at amusement parks, it's almost impossible to break out of these tracks once you're strapped in. Very few children go through low-level math in middle school and suddenly leap forward into Algebra II and Calculus.

Ridiculously enough, it's often the low-level math courses that are the most practical and useful. Business math tends to include balance sheets, measurement, graphing, and many other handy skills that could very well benefit an academic-track student.

The main problem, though, is with those students who want to attend college and find at the last minute that their math education is inadequate. Most college guides will alert you to the number of math credits required by colleges and universities. It makes sense to look at these guides long before your child is ready to apply.

According to *Everybody Counts: A Report to the Nation on the Future of Mathematics Education*, nearly 60 percent of college math enrollments are in remedial courses—essentially high school math. Should you be spending tuition money on courses that your children should have had for free in public school? Only half of the high school students in the United States take more than two years of high school math.

Stay alert to your child's curriculum and the way it dovetails over the years with college requirements. Ask about tracking, and don't let teachers and administrators pooh-pooh your concerns. You need to know if your child's future is being compromised by a system that limits his or her options.

31.

Understand that Mere Computation Isn't Enough

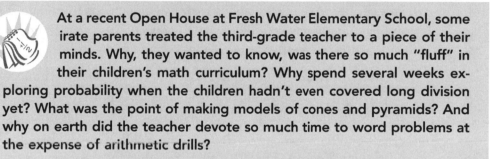

At a recent Open House at Fresh Water Elementary School, some irate parents treated the third-grade teacher to a piece of their minds. Why, they wanted to know, was there so much "fluff" in their children's math curriculum? Why spend several weeks exploring probability when the children hadn't even covered long division yet? What was the point of making models of cones and pyramids? And why on earth did the teacher devote so much time to word problems at the expense of arithmetic drills?

The goal of math education is not to make your child a human calculator. Calculators are cheap and efficient, and anyone can learn to use one. Learning to add, subtract, multiply, and divide is important, yes—in the same way that learning the alphabet and the rudiments of grammar is important. These skills are not an end in themselves; they are building blocks.

The National Research Council's report on the future of mathematics education mentions geometry, measurement, estimation, statistics, and probability as vital skills for everyone. The report also isolates some mathematical modes of thought that should be considered goals for math education, including these:

Modeling, which is the ability to represent "worldly phenomena by mental constructs, often visual or symbolic." Graphing changes over time or drawing a room to scale are examples of modeling.

Optimization, which is the ability to find the most efficient or least expensive solution by asking "what if" and exploring the possibilities. Most of the problem solving we do as adults involves optimization of one sort or another.

Inference, which is the ability to draw conclusions from data, including from incomplete or inconsistent sources. To be informed voters, we need to be good at this skill.

Logical analysis, which is the ability to understand the implications of given hypotheses and to explain observations by generalizing. Babies do this when they recognize that those flying creatures are all birds, but that not all things that fly are birds. Scientists perform logical analyses every day of their working lives.

The goal of math education, according to the study, should be to develop a "capacity of mind that enables one to read critically, to identify fallacies, to detect bias, to assess risk, and to suggest alternatives." This may seem like heavy stuff to those of us who are just now helping our youngsters understand "take away," but it's a desirable objective. If our aim is simply to create calculators, we might as well forget the "love" of mathematics we're claiming to foster. A better goal is to lead children to think mathematically, to help them use math intelligently to reach their own goals.

Many sections of this book suggest activities that are designed to stimulate mathematical modes of thought. Here are some examples:

Modeling: See #3, #4, #7, #39, #40

Optimization: See #34, #35, #36, #37, #38, #39, #40

Inference: See #16, #17

Logical Analysis: See #6, #12, #36, #37

32.

Adjust Your Expectations Upward

My friend Nan used to write her kids' term papers. When she admitted that to me, my first reaction was profound jealousy. In my 17 years of schooling, my parents never so much as painted a salt-and-flour map for me. Where did I go wrong?

My chief reaction, however, was confusion. Call me naive, but it had never occurred to me that parents did such things. Nan's kids were very bright, unusually so. I would have recognized that even if I hadn't known that they got good grades. But what in the world did those grades mean, if Mom did the work? Who was being graded?

Nan was surprised at my surprise. She saw nothing weird about her contribution to her children's portfolios. "That school gives too much homework," she explained. "There's no way they can do it all."

So Nan, who worked a 9-to-5 job, went home, cooked dinner, washed the dishes, and did her kids' homework.

Study after study has shown that parents' expectations that their children will succeed, attend college, and have satisfying careers correlate impressively with those children's actual achievements. Making it clear to your children that you expect great things from them is one of the most important things you can do for their education.

Whether or not a school has tracking (see #30), students are nearly always consigned to tracks in their teachers' minds. If a teacher considers a child deficient and slow, that child will almost invariably fail. If the teacher thinks a child is capable and bright, that child will do as well as he or she possibly can. It's not hard to understand why this happens. Teachers typically call on the children they consider capable of answering their questions. The other children may begin by waving their hands, but eventually they learn not to bother. They lose interest because their interest is not supported.

You need to combat the self-fulfilling prophecy that allows teachers to predict early on who will succeed and who will fail. It's vital that your children know that you believe in their potential and that mediocrity is not an option.

Think about the messages you give your children as they struggle with their homework. Do you do their work for them? You're saying, "You can't do it." Do you complain about careless errors? You're saying, "Smart people don't make mistakes." Do you simply ask whether they did their work without asking to see it? You're saying, "Your work doesn't interest me." Do you give them additional homework beyond what they get from their teachers? You're saying, "You can't learn in school."

The messages you want to be sending are quite different. You want your children to know that they *can* do it; that *everyone* makes mistakes, but smart people recognize them; that you are very much interested in the work they do; and that they *can* learn in school, despite such obstacles as outdated textbooks and overworked teachers. Besides bolstering your children's self-esteem, you are helping to build competent, independent, successful adults. Isn't that your real assignment?

33.

Recognize Differences Among Children

"It makes no sense at all," complains a parent I know. "Our oldest is a total math whiz. He's certain to get all the math prizes in his senior year, and he's a shoo-in at M.I.T. The middle kid is probably going to be an engineer or architect if we can get her off the computer long enough to think about a career. But the youngest? We're lucky he can add and subtract. He's a terrific writer, but numbers leave him completely cold. I swear we raised them the same way—what happened?"

It's tempting to compare kids. We all do it. As my daughter plays with her friends, we parents sit around admiring one child's ability to share and another's clever ball handling. We know that children develop differently and at different rates, but there's always a voice in the back of our heads saying, "Shouldn't she be able to do that? How come he's so good at it and she's not?"

You may hear that little voice often as one child seems to lag behind his or her friends or siblings: "Why can't Mikey count to 10 yet? How come Julie can't add as well as Kyle?"

This kind of comparative analysis is unproductive. Even if you don't voice your anxiety, your children will sense it. The child who is good at math will feel self-conscious, and the child who is not will feel stupid.

Even within a single family, children often differ widely in development, attention span, likes, and dislikes. You need to recognize that fact and learn to appreciate those differences. If you don't, your children will suffer.

Instead of getting agitated about children's differences, cherish their special traits. Be glad that Mikey can play roly-poly and build splendid Lego® towers; his dexterity with objects will certainly help him with math later on. Celebrate the fact that Julie is musical and already plays "Dark Brown Is the River" better than you can. Her grasp of the patterns and logic of music will allow her to see mathematical patterns and logic better than some of her classmates ever will.

As described in detail in #18, children must take a discrete series of prerequisite steps before they are able to grasp specific math skills. Every child takes the same steps, but no two children take them at the same time. Mikey will almost certainly count to ten soon, and his slow progress to that mastery doesn't mean he'll be slow in math forever. Julie may not add as well as Kyle because it took her longer to recognize that a single number names the same amount no matter how that amount is arranged. Now that she's grasped that concept, she may well fly past Kyle by the time they reach beginning multiplication.

Remember, too, that you can't force children to love something just because you want them too. It doesn't work with vegetables, and it won't work with math. The best you can do is to show by example how much fun math can be and hope that your enthusiasm rubs off on your kids.

SECTION 4

Focus on
Specific Skills

34.

Problem Solving: Choose the Operation

Trevor saved the change from his bridge tolls every week for 3 weeks. Now he has collected $2.55. How much did he save each week?

Trevor wants to spend his saved change on a car wash that costs $3.00. How much more money does he need?

Where Trevor lives, tax is 7 cents on the dollar. How much tax will Trevor have to pay for his $3.00 car wash?

With tax, how much will Trevor spend in all?

D o your eyes glaze over when you see problems like these? Many people who suffer from math anxiety are made especially anxious by word problems. Each problem is different, and no obvious signs exist to tell you what to do to reach a solution.

Most word problems require the performance of one or more operations: addition, subtraction, multiplication, or division. Knowing which operation is called for is the key to solving the problem.

Addition is the first operation children learn in school and perhaps the most intuitive—even a baby understands the concept of *more*. Addition is used to combine groups or to increase a number of objects. In word problems, the need to add is often indicated by the clue words *in all, total,* or *all together.*

Subtraction is the inverse of addition. It has two primary purposes: to decrease a whole number of objects (take away) or to compare numbers of objects. Words that signify subtraction in a word problem might include *how many are left, how much more,* or *how much less.*

Multiplication involves the combination of numerically similar groups of objects. As in addition, multiplication of whole numbers involves an increase, so the words *in all* or *all together* may apply to multiplication as well. The word *of,* as in "You have 3 cartons of 12 eggs each," is also a clue that multiplication is involved.

Division, the inverse of multiplication, is used to separate like groups of objects. The word *each* may indicate that division is required.

To solve any word problem, you need to read carefully and then decide:

What do I know?   What is the question?   What is the answer?

Okay, now look back at Trevor's problem, which is a multistep problem that calls for multiple operations on a variety of numbers. In the first part, you learn the following information:

You know that: Trevor has $2.55. He collected it over 3 weeks.

The question is: How much money did he collect each week (in 1 week)?

Even if the clue word *each* didn't suggest division, you could think:
The answer is: An amount of money that is less than $2.55. Because Trevor got $2.55 in 3 weeks, in 1 week he must get $2.55 ÷ 3, or <u>$.85</u>.

Now try the next part:
You know that: Trevor has $2.55. He wants a car wash that costs $3.00.

The question is: How much more money does he need?

You can tell by looking at the numbers that Trevor has less than he needs. You *could* solve the problem by adding on to $2.55 until you reached $3.00, but the easier path is to use the inverse operation: subtraction.

The answer is: An amount of money that is less than $3.00. Trevor already has $2.55, so he must need $3.00 – $2.55, or <u>$.45</u>.

Alas, poor Trevor hasn't figured in the bane of every penny-pinching consumer—the tax. In his case, tax is 7 percent, which is to say that for every dollar he spends, he pays an extra 7 cents to the government.

You know that: The car wash costs $3.00. Tax is 7 cents per dollar.

The question is: How much tax will Trevor pay?

In this situation, like amounts are being combined. You *could* solve it by adding 7 + 7 + 7, but it's faster to use the operation designed to take the place of repeated addition: multiplication.

The answer is: An amount of money that is less than $3.00. Tax is 7 cents per dollar, and there are 3 dollars in all, so $3 \times 7 =$ <u>21 cents</u>.

The final question includes the words *in all*, which should tell you automatically to add or multiply.

You know that: The car wash costs $3.00. Additional tax is $.21.

The question is: How much will Trevor spend in all?

It's clear that the amounts being considered are not numerically similar, so multiplication is out of the question.

The answer is: An amount of money that is greater than $3.00. The additional tax is $.21, so $3.00 + $.21 = <u>$3.21</u>.

Once you have evaluated the problem, looked for clue words, and chosen the correct operation to use, the rest is a matter of doing the arithmetic, for which you can always use a calculator.

How to Practice Choosing the Operation

Use children's math texts. Skip around from chapter to chapter and find a variety of word problems. Read them aloud and have children state what they know and what the question is. Work with them to determine whether the problems call for addition, subtraction, multiplication, or division. Discuss any clue words that helped them decide. Don't bother solving the problems at this point.

Use a grocery circular to devise problems of your own. For example, if cans of olives are on sale for 59 cents, how much will 4 cans cost? Ask your child to determine the operation that will most easily solve the problems.

Using the same circular, ask children to make up one problem for each operation: addition, subtraction, multiplication, and division.

Return to Trevor's problem and have children suggest extensions. For example, Trevor has only $2.55, how much more will he need to buy the car wash with tax? Can he buy it with next week's change?

In real life, problem solving is the most practical everyday use of mathematics. When you fill out your tax forms or make change in a transaction, the math you're doing could be stated as a word problem. It's much more likely in real life that you'll face a question such as "How much is left?" than that you'll come across a written equation such as $34 - 5 = ?$ Fear of word problems is easily overcome through practice and the recognition that they are simply verbal versions of real-life situations involving numbers.

91A 5351

ACCORDING TO MY CALCULATIONS
THE PROBLEM DOESN'T EXIST

35.

Problem Solving: Guess and Check

Tuition at your local college is three times what it was when you were in school. You paid $5,280 a year. What is the tuition today?

Many problems don't require an exact answer. You can find a ballpark answer by rounding numbers and estimating, and often that answer is good enough. A useful strategy for getting close to the exact answer is called Guess and Check, sometimes called Test and Check.

To use Guess and Check to solve the tuition problem, you follow these steps:

You know that: Tuition in your day was $5,280 a year. Tuition today is 3 times that amount.

The question is: How much is tuition today?

The word *times* is a pretty good clue that multiplication is involved. Using Guess and Check, you can round and plug in any guess that seems reasonable as the answer, say, $15,000. Then you check:

$3 \times$ tuition = $15,000

tuition = $5,000

Your guess is too low.

So try another guess, say, $18,000.

$3 \times$ tuition = $18,000

tuition = $6,000

Your guess is too high.

You now know that the answer lies somewhere between $15,000 and $18,000, which may be all you need to know. (The exact answer, as it turns out, is $15,840.)

This strategy is especially helpful in multistep problems. Suppose you were given the problem stated this way:

Tuition at your local college has gone up by $580 a year for the last five years. Five years ago, tuition was $12,940. What is tuition today?

There are many ways to solve the problem, but Guess and Check allows you to come close with an estimate. The more complicated the problem, the more likely you may be to choose Guess and Check as a problem-solving strategy.

How to Practice Guessing and Checking

Use children's blocks or beads. Make a pattern with them; for example, square, circle, circle, square, circle, circle. Ask children to guess and check how many of each shape you would need to build a chain of 10, 25, or 50 blocks or beads.

Use the calendar as a tool. Ask children to guess and check the amount of allowance they will receive in 2, 14, and 28 weeks, or between now and December 31. Have them guess and check how many days or weeks lie between the date today and each child's next birthday.

36.

Problem Solving: Use Smaller Numbers

> You are looking at two houses. One costs $147,630, and the other costs $124,750. The cheaper one has 2,500 square feet, and the more expensive one has 3,700 square feet. Judging just by cost per square foot, which is the better buy?

Problems with many large numbers can be daunting. You often can't see past the gigantic numbers to determine which operation to use to solve the problem. The easiest way to get past this stumbling block is to imagine the problem with different, smaller, made-up numbers. When you use smaller numbers, you don't have to make the problem make sense. You don't even have to use numbers that are in proportion to the numbers in the problem. The goal is to remove the obstacle to your understanding of the problem. Once you've done that, you can go back and solve, using the original numbers.

To use smaller numbers with this housing problem, you might think: You are looking at two houses. One costs $40, and the other costs $20. The cheaper one has 2 square feet, and the more expensive one has 3 square feet. Judging just by cost per square foot, which is the better buy?

The question is: Which is the better buy?

Substituting the ridiculous smaller numbers for the actual numbers in the problem lets you see that the problem is a comparison between costs per square foot. You can tell that you have to divide square footage into price for each house and then compare the two answers.

Now you can go back to the original problem:

The answer is: One of the houses.

For the expensive house: $147,630 ÷ 3,700 = $39.90/sq. ft.

For the cheaper house: $124,750 ÷ 2,500 = $49.90/sq. ft.

Therefore, <u>the more expensive house</u> is the better buy.

(Granted, this is a pretty stupid way to buy a house.)

This technique works well for any situation in which the operation to use is not immediately obvious. For example, suppose you are asked to restate this fraction as a decimal:

$$\frac{35.38}{61}$$

By referring immediately to a simpler, smaller number, you can easily see that division is the operation to use:

$$\frac{1}{4}$$

Think: Divide 4 into 1 to get the decimal equivalent 0.25. Therefore, to get the decimal equivalent for the first fraction, you must divide 61 into 35.38, yielding <u>0.58</u>.

How to Practice Using Smaller Numbers

Use newspaper ads for big-ticket items such as automobiles. Have children practice dropping off the last three digits of the price and restating it as a one- or two-digit number. They can then compare "prices" to see which car costs more. For example, a car listed at $22,500 would be $22, and one listed at $18,750 would be $18.

On index cards, write down a variety of dates from a single century—for example, 1865, 1812, 1890, and 1898. Have children drop off the first two digits to put the numbers in order from least to greatest.

Make up problems in this format, using four- to seven-digit numbers, and have children use smaller numbers to tell you which operation to use to solve them:

Over _____ snowflakes fell on our house yesterday, and _____ fell today. How many fell in all? How many more fell today than yesterday? *(addition, subtraction)* Santa carried _____ sacks of _____ gifts each on his trip around the world. He delivered gifts to _____ homes. How many gifts were there all together? How many gifts went to each home? *(multiplication, division)*

37.

Problem Solving: Find an Easier Problem

You're traveling from home to Grandmother's house, 250 miles away. You plan to leave home at 8:00 a.m. and travel half the distance to Grandmother's before stopping for a 1-hour break at Estes Park. Assuming you average 50 miles per hour while moving, at what time will you reach the park? At what time will you reach Grandmother's house?

In a multistep problem like the preceding one, it's all too easy to get lost in calculations and forget the original question. The best strategy for such a problem is to break it down into pieces, to find the series of simpler problems that lead to the final solution.

You could Find an Easier Problem from one of several directions. Here are some examples:

Easier Problem #1: You're traveling 250 miles. You average 50 miles per hour. How long will it take to go 250 miles?

Easier Problem #2: Grandmother's house is 250 miles away. Estes Park is half that distance away. How many miles is it to Estes Park?

Easier Problem #3: You're traveling x miles to Estes Park, averaging 50 miles per hour. How long does the trip take?

Easier Problem #4: The distance between home and Estes Park takes *y* hours to drive. The distance between Estes Park and Grandmother's house takes *y* hours, too. You spend 1 hour at the park. How much time do you spend on the road?

Easier Problem #5: You leave the house at 8:00 a.m. and travel for *y* hours to Estes Park. At what time do you arrive?

Easier Problem #6: You leave the house at 8:00 a.m. and travel for *y* hours to the park, spend 1 hour there, and continue for *y* additional hours. At what time do you arrive at Grandmother's?

Problem #1 is a simple division problem:
$250 \div 50 = 5$ hours

Problem #2 is also a simple division problem:
$250 \div 2 = 125$ miles

Problem #3 requires the answer to Problem #2:
$125 \div 50 = 2.5$ hours

Problem #4 requires the answer to Problem #3:
$2.5 + 1 + 2.5 = 6$ hours

Problem #5 requires the answer to Problem #3:
8:00 a.m. + 2.5 hours = 10:30 a.m.

Problem #6 requires the answer to Problem #3:
8:00 a.m. + 2.5 hours + 1 hour + 2.5 hours = 2 p.m.

Or Problem #6 requires the answer to Problem #4:
8:00 a.m. + 6 hours = 2:00 p.m.

Now return to the original problem:

The answer is: Two times of day.

For the first question: see Problem #5—<u>10:30 a.m.</u>

For the second question: see Problem #6—<u>2:00 p.m.</u>

Not every multistep problem requires this deliberate breakdown of parts; most of these steps can be done in your head once you understand the problem. However, this is a good strategy for children to use when they're put off by complicated problems, or when analysis of their errors (see #23) shows that they tend to answer some portion of a word problem and not the whole thing.

How to Practice Finding an Easier Problem

Use a road map that includes mileage. Make up a fantasy road trip from one place to another that includes stops at several towns. Have children determine the mileage between each pair of towns and add to find the total miles traveled.

Have children use the ages of each member of your family. Ask them to find the difference in ages between each pair of family members. Which age difference is greatest? Which is least?

38.

Problem Solving: Work Backward

You deposited $1,200 in the bank during the month of January. You then wrote checks—$500 for rent, $180 for utilities, and $225 for miscellaneous other expenses. Now your bank account shows a total of $975. How much did you have in the bank at the beginning of January?

There are many ways to solve this problem, but one useful way is to work backward from the final $975. Instead of subtracting your expenses, you can add them back to the amount left, using addition as the inverse operation of subtraction:

$975 + $225 + $180 + $500 = $1,880

Now return to the original problem:

The question is: How much did you have before the deposit was made?

The answer is: An amount of money not including the deposit.

You see from working backward that you started out with $1,880 before your expenses. Subtracting your deposit gives you the amount you had before that deposit was made:

$1,880 − $1,200 = $680

The Work Backward strategy is useful for determining original amounts of money, determining original times (for example, when should you wake up if you have to be somewhere by noon and it takes x hours to get ready and travel there?), or comparing amounts over time.

How to Practice Working Backward

- Use a grocery store circular. Tell children that they have $10 left after shopping. Have them circle five items they "bought" and determine how much money they took to the store with them originally.

- Give children today's date and a date earlier in the year. Remind them of the number of days in each month. Ask them to determine how many days have passed between the dates.

- For older children, name a salary figure for children's make-believe jobs. Explain that last year's salary was 10 percent less, and have them determine last year's salary. Continue back for several years.

39.

Problem Solving: Make a List

You arrive at your vacation spot with 2 T-shirts, 2 pairs of shorts, 1 pair of running shoes, and 1 pair of sandals. How many different outfits can you wear while you are there?

Some people approach a problem like this numerically; I'm not one of them. When I see a "combination" type of problem, I immediately make a list.

1. T-shirt A, shorts A, running shoes
2. T-shirt A, shorts A, sandals
3. T-shirt A, shorts B, running shoes
4. T-shirt A, shorts B, sandals
5. T-shirt B, shorts A, running shoes
6. T-shirt B, shorts A, sandals
7. T-shirt B, shorts B, running shoes
8. T-shirt B, shorts B, sandals

Now return to the original problem:

The question is: How many outfits can you wear?

The answer is: A number of outfits. The list shows you <u>8</u> different combinations of clothing and footwear.

Oddly, many children, faced with a simple problem of this nature, feel that it's somehow cheating to draw a picture or doodle a list on their scratch paper. While it's certainly less efficient than multiplying $2 \times 2 \times 2$, making a list is far better than staring dully at a problem, hoping the solution will magically appear.

The key to making a list is to organize it. Notice that in my list, I begin with all the combinations that start with T-shirt A and shorts A. I could have made a list that started like this:

1. T-shirt A, shorts A, running shoes

2. T-shirt B, shorts A, sandals

However, it would have been an inefficient way of looking at the problem. By organizing my list, I ensure that I don't skip any combinations.

Another way to make a list for combination problems is to use a tree diagram. Counting the ends of the branches gives the number and form of all your possible combinations:

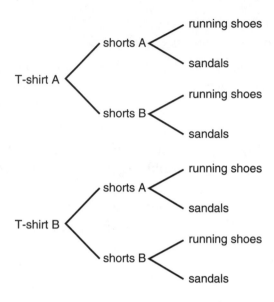

How to Practice Making a List

🖉 Give children two pairs of shoes and ask them to list all the ways they could put shoes from the pairs on their feet—for example, running shoe on left foot, sandal on right foot.

🖉 Have children name their three favorite ice cream flavors and make a list showing all the different ways they might make a triple-scoop ice cream cone.

Ask children to list the various ways they could show a given amount of money with coins. For example, 17 cents could be 1 dime, 1 nickel, 2 pennies; 1 dime, 7 pennies; 1 nickel, 12 pennies; 2 nickels, 7 pennies; 3 nickels, 2 pennies; or 17 pennies.

40.
Problem Solving: Draw a Picture or Diagram

Loretta and her husband have invited 3 couples to dinner. Loretta believes that etiquette dictates that couples not sit side by side at the table. She and her husband will sit at the ends of their rectangular table, and 3 guests will sit on each side. How might they be arranged?

In high society, people have special place cards for determining solutions to problems like these. You can play around with the cards until you find a combination that works. However, you don't need a fancy prop; you can simply draw your own diagram.

Loretta   Loretta's husband

Now return to the original problem:

The question is: How might people be arranged so that no couple sits together?

The answer is: An arrangement of people. The diagram presented here shows one possibility.

This is one of those problems that has more than one solution but that can easily be complicated by adding variables. What if you didn't want couples to face each other, either? What if you wanted the table to run boy, girl, boy, girl?

Drawing a picture or diagram can help you see exactly what's going on in a problem. It's one of the problem-solving strategies most useful in so-called "real life," applicable especially to situations that involve combinations, as here, or those that involve measurements.

How to Practice Drawing a Picture or Diagram

- Give children a measuring tape and graph paper and have them determine whether the furniture in one room could fit into a second room. How would the furniture have to be arranged in the second room?

- Display a can and ask children to determine how many cans would be on the bottom row of a pyramid of 21, 28, and 36 cans (6, 7, 8). Then ask children to determine how many cans in all would be in pyramids with 3, 4, and 5 cans in the bottom row (6, 10, 15). Ask children to make up more can-pyramid problems.

- Ask children to draw pictures showing how many heel-toe footsteps it takes to walk the length of a hallway. Then have them test their drawings by acting out the problem.

41.

Mental Arithmetic: Estimate

You call Fabulous Furnace Repair to inspect your broken furnace. The workers come out to the house, make a mess, and leave you with a written estimate: The job will take so many person-hours and require a new nozzle at this price and new ductwork at that price. It's up to you to determine whether the estimate is fair and reasonable, or whether you want to get a second opinion.

*E*stimation, or approximate calculation, is probably the most important of all math skills. The ability to glance at a problem and make an educated guess at a ballpark solution is useful no matter what you do for a living.

Estimation is hard to teach, and it's generally taught badly. Children spend a long time in school learning to round numbers to the nearest ten, hundred, thousand, and so on, without really knowing why they're bothering to do so.

Rounding is important, but it isn't an end in itself, which too often is how it's presented. Here are some examples of rounding: If you know that a loaf of bread calls for $2\frac{3}{4}$ cups of flour, you can round that up to 3 cups and determine that you ought to have on hand about 6 cups in all if you want to bake two loaves. A child rounds to the nearest whole number when he says, "I'm almost 8 years old." You round when you give the pizza delivery guy $20 for a $16.50 order.

If you round numbers sensibly, you can estimate sensible solutions. Suppose you want to estimate how much a person makes in a year if her take-home pay is $1,238.75 per month. Rounding to the nearest whole number gives you $1,239, which is still a tough number to work with. You might be better off rounding to the nearest thousand, because $1,000 is easier to multiply by 12 months in a year. However, the answer, $12,000, may not be as accurate as you want. Rounding to the nearest hundred, $1,200, gives you a closer estimate: $1,200 × 12 = <u>$14,400</u>.

Here are some situations for which you might choose to estimate instead of finding an exact answer:

- Determining the tip for a cab ride
- Judging the length of time it takes to get to the airport
- Telling your boss when a report will be finished
- Comparing the costs of appliances in several stores
- Choosing the most likely of four answers on the SAT exam

About this last item: Many multiple-choice exams, and the SAT is no exception, rely on children's inability to estimate. The distractors (wrong choices) are likely to be off by a factor of 10 or 100, in hopes of tricking the child who can do the arithmetic but has lost the sense of the problem. Here's an example:

Janet invested $7,200, part at 4% and the rest at 5%. If she received the same annual income from both investments, what was her total annual income from the two investments?

A. $160

B. $320

C. $4,000

D. $3,200

E. $7,200

Without even getting into the arithmetic at all, a child should be able to eliminate answers C, D, and E simply because there's no way that 4 percent and 5 percent of $7,200 could yield such high amounts. In fact, had Janet invested the whole thing at the higher percentage, she could have made only $360. Had she invested the whole thing at the lower percentage, she would have made $288. The answer, therefore, must be <u>B</u>. (For more about reasonable answers, see #43.) Notice that you don't have to work through the problem; you just have to understand it. On a timed test, the ability to estimate can save precious minutes and add precious points to the final score.

There are places where precision is called for. You wouldn't want an architect or a nuclear engineer to measure in round numbers. However, as most of us go about our daily routines, there are dozens of times when estimation can give us a speedy, close-enough response to a complex problem.

Some Words to Use When Estimating

about	approximately
around	nearly
less than	between
more than	in round numbers

How to Practice Estimating

Offer your children a certain amount per hour to do a given household job. Challenge them to estimate the time it will take and to present you with a written estimate of the cost of the job.

As you prepare a meal together, ask children to restate precise cookbook measurements as approximate measurements. Determine together whether the estimates are close enough to make the recipe work.

Use your children's math textbooks. Pick word problems at random and ask children to estimate answers. Discuss whether an approximate answer would be good enough or whether precision is called for in each case.

42.

Mental Arithmetic: Calculate in Your Head

At the hair salon, your cut and style costs $25. You want to tip the stylist 20%. How much will you pay in all?

It would be awfully tiresome to have to drag out a calculator for every transaction like the one described here. It's far better to be comfortable enough with basic math skills so that you can calculate such answers in your head.

The nice thing about doing calculations in your head is that eventually you learn shortcuts. If you were to solve the preceding problem on paper, you might write:

$$\$25 + (.20(\$25)) = \$25 + \$5 = \underline{\$30}$$

or

$$\$25 \times \frac{20}{100} = \frac{\$500}{100} = \$5$$

$$\$5 + \$25 = \underline{\$30}$$

When you do the same problem in your head, you don't have time or mental space for such fancy calculations. You need to think:

Ten percent of $25 is $2.50. Twice that is $5. $5 + $25 = <u>$30</u>

    or

Twenty percent is the same as one-fifth. One-fifth of $25 is $5. $5 + $25 = <u>$30</u>

    To do calculations in your head, you must be fairly fluent with arithmetic basics—you need to know your multiplication tables, for example. It helps to know some shortcut tricks as well.

Some Tips for Multiplying Quickly

times 2: Think "Double."

$$7 \times 2 = \text{double } 7 = \underline{14}$$

times 3: Think "Double, double, minus 1."

$$7 \times 2 = 14 \times 2 = 28 - 7 = \underline{21}$$

times 4: Think "Double, double."

$$7 \times 2 = 14 \times 2 = \underline{28}$$

times 5: Think "Times 10, then half."

$$7 \times 10 = 70 \times \tfrac{1}{2} = \underline{35}$$

times 6: Think "Times 3, then double."

$$7 \times 3 = 21 \times 2 = \underline{42}$$

times 7: Think "Double, double, double, minus 1."

$$7 \times 2 = 14 \times 2 = 28 \times 2 = 56 - 7 = \underline{49}$$

times 8: Think "Double, double, double."

$$7 \times 2 = 14 \times 2 = 28 \times 2 = \underline{56}$$

times 9: Think "Times 10, minus 1."

$$7 \times 10 = 70 - 7 = \underline{63}$$

Some Shortcuts for Calculating in Your Head

🖉 Look for tens. For example, to add the string of numbers 2 + 8 + 7 + 6 + 4, add the numbers that make tens first: 10 + 7 + 10. The sum, 27, is then easy to calculate.

🖉 Look for doubles. For example, to add the string of numbers 8 + 4 + 9 + 8, adding 8 + 8 first may help. Then 16 + 13 = 29 is easier to see. (Or think 16 + 4 = 20, 20 + 9 = 29.)

🖉 Look for whole numbers. Suppose you're adding these measurements: $\frac{3}{4}$ in. + $\frac{1}{2}$ in. + $3\frac{1}{4}$ in. Adding $\frac{3}{4}$ to $3\frac{1}{4}$ gets you a whole number, 4. Then you can easily see that the answer is $4\frac{1}{2}$ in.

🖉 Base your percentages on 10%. A simple shift in decimal point gets you 10% of any number. Doubling that answer gives you 20%, because 20% = 2 × 10%. To find 15% of $40, for example, you would find 10%, or $4. The additional 5% would be half of that, or $2, for a total of $6.

How to Practice Calculating in Your Head

🖉 Make a game of adding strings of one-digit numbers. Start by giving four numbers, one at a time, so that children have time to add after each. Because it's more efficient to find doubles or tens, move on to giving four numbers all at once. Once children have mastered that, have them add five and six numbers. Continue with two-digit numbers, having children estimate the sum (see #41).

🖉 When children accompany you to the grocery store, have them keep a running estimate in their heads of the total you will spend on groceries. Compare their estimates with the final receipt.

Ask older children to find the tip on a $10 meal, a $15 meal, and so on, if you tip 15 percent or 20 percent. Suggest that they make you a list to refer to when the family dines out.

43.

Mental Arithmetic: Determine Reasonable Answers

The ratio of males to females in your extended family is 3 to 2. If there are 33 males, how many people in all are in your extended family?

A. 32

B. 22

C. 55

D. 99

E. Cannot be determined from the information given

Children are regularly faced with multiple-choice questions like this one. In real life, we are rarely given such choices; we usually struggle to find answers based solely on the information in the original problem.

Whether you're working on an achievement test at school or a presentation at work, it's important to recognize whether your answer is reasonable. To do that, it's vital to remember the question being asked.

You know that: The ratio of males to females is 3 to 2. There are 33 males.

The question is: How many males and females are there in all?

Given these facts, what do you know about the answer?

The answer is: A number greater than 33, because it will include both males and females.

Look what that knowledge makes possible: You can toss out answers A and B already! They are not reasonable, because both are less than the answer you expect.

What else do you know about the answer?

The answer is: A number less than 66. If the ratio were 3 to 3, the number of females would be the same as the number of males, and there would be 66 people in all. Because the ratio is 3 to 2, you expect there to be fewer females than males, so the answer must be less than 66.

Okay, now you can eliminate answer D. It is not reasonable, because it is greater than the answer you expect.

At this point, you are probably clear that the answer is C. To check it, plug in the numbers:

Total = 55

Number of males = 33

Number of females = 55 − 33 = 22

Ratio of 33 to 22 = 3 to 2

The answer is <u>C</u>.

The classic example of a problem in which reasonable answers make all the difference is the "bus trip" problem:

250 children are traveling on a field trip to Washington, D.C. Each bus can hold a maximum of 30 students. How many buses are needed?

Do you see why "$8\frac{1}{3}$" or "8 remainder 10" is not a reasonable answer? Yet all too many children look at such a problem, do the arithmetic blindly, and are confused when the answer is marked wrong. The correct answer has to be <u>9 buses</u>. This kind of mistake is one reason teachers are so adamant that children include units in their answers. Writing "$8\frac{1}{3}$ buses" would tip most students off to the silliness of their answer.

Here's another example of an unreasonable answer:

You're calculating your profit for the month of March.

Your income was $1,832, and your expenses were $1,945.

You determine that your profit was $113.

It's all too typical that, when faced with a problem like this one, children (and adults, too) simply subtract the smaller number from the larger one. Unfortunately, a closer reading of the problem shows that your income was the smaller number. Because profit equals income minus expenses, the real answer is a negative number, –<u>$113</u>.

Some Questions that Help Determine Reasonable Answers

- Is the answer too small or too large to make sense?

- Should the answer be a fraction or a whole number?

- Should the answer be a positive or a negative number?

How to Practice Determining Reasonable Answers

- Use your local newspaper. Read aloud a brief article that contains numbers, but leave the numbers out. Ask children to supply numbers that seem realistic. If you need to, begin by supplying choices and asking whether they are reasonable. Discuss why the unreasonable choices are unreasonable.

Example: Voters in Freeville today reelected their mayor and village council. Most of the voters in this tiny village, a total of _____, turned out to vote. They also approved a $_____ raise for the part-time village clerk and a _____% hike in village taxes.

Have children suggest reasonable prices for grocery items. (Many politicians have tried and failed on this one!) Check their suggestions against grocery circulars.

Ask children to invent questions for which the reasonable answer might be 10; 100; 1,000; and 10,000.

> *Examples:*
>
>> How many people fit in a minivan?
>>
>> How many people came to our band concert?
>>
>> How many students go to our high school?
>>
>> How many people fit into the stadium?

Have children make up questions for which the answer could be a fraction and questions for which the answer could never be a fraction.

> *Examples:*
>
>> How tall is the flag on the merry-go-round?
>>
>> How many people rode the merry-go-round?

Have children guess and check (see #35) the distance between two points in the room or two trees outdoors. Discuss whether their initial guess was reasonable.

44.

Spatial Visualization: Extend and Predict Patterns

What is the next figure in this pattern?

♣ ◆ ♣ ◆ ♣ <u>?</u>

Boys do better than girls on test items requiring spatial visualization. It seems clear, however, that with adequate instruction, girls can make up that gender difference. One of the suggested reasons for that initial gap is that boys are given more hands-on building and manipulating experiences at a young age. Whatever the truth is, both boys and girls can profit from work with spatial visualization; it can help them with geometry, intelligence tests, and real-life problem solving.

Spatial visualization can be as simple as looking at the figure

⬜

and recognizing that even though it's printed in two dimensions, it represents something three-dimensional. You then should be able to compare that shape in your mind with real-life objects and determine which objects have the same qualities—for example, a box, a television set, or an ice cube.

Spatial visualization may involve predictive skills. When you look at the shapes for the pattern problem, you need to recognize the pattern in order to predict the next item.

You know that: The shapes go in this order from left to right: club, diamond, club, diamond, club.

The question is: What comes next?

If your spatial visualization skills are weak, saying the pattern aloud can help.

The answer is: One of the two shapes. Because each shape appears once in each two-shape pair, and because the other pairs have a diamond after each club, the answer must be ♦.

The ability to see and predict patterns is a skill that helps you in areas from architecture and art to accounting and agriculture. You've seen how children can be encouraged to find patterns in everyday objects (see #12). You can help them improve their predictive skills with a variety of games like those described here.

How to Practice Extending and Predicting Patterns

Use playing cards. Lay out a pattern involving color, suit, or face value and have children tell what comes next. Ask children to take turns creating their own patterns and having other family members tell what's next.

Examples:

Easy   ♣ ♦ ♣ ♦ ♣ ? (♦)

Harder   ♣ ♣ ♦ ♥ ♣ ♣ ♦ ♥ ♣ ♣ ♦ ? (♥)

Hardest   10♣ J♦ Q♥ 10♦ J♥ Q♣ 10♥ ? (J♣)

Take turns using blocks, Lincoln Logs®, or Lego® to build walls with repeating patterns. Describe each other's patterns.

Use an article of clothing with a distinct pattern, such as stripes, plaid, or a repeating print. Ask children to determine what would show next if the clothing continued below the hem. (You can do the same exercise with repeating patterns on wrapping paper.)

45.

Spatial Visualization: Recognize Translations, Reflections, and Rotations

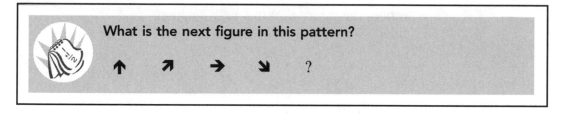

What is the next figure in this pattern?

↑   ↗   →   ↘   ?

To paraphrase Gertrude Stein, a square is a square is a square. Just because it changes size or location, its fundamental qualities are not altered. Very young children don't recognize this fact (see #18), but as they grow and gain experience, they learn that these are all the same shape:

■   ▪   ◆

Spatial visualization includes three concepts that involve a change in position of a figure in space:

 In a *translation,* the figure *slides* to a new position.

✎ In a *rotation,* the figure *turns* to a new position.

✎ In a *reflection,* the figure *flips* to a new position.

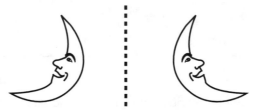

Engineers, graphic designers, landscape architects, and photographers use these concepts every day. Coordinate geometry requires students to understand the concepts. In addition, intelligence tests often feature questions based on translations, rotations, and reflections. A typical question might resemble the one posed earlier about the order of the arrows.

You know that: The shapes go in this order from left to right: arrow up, arrow 45° right, arrow 90° right, arrow 135° right.

The question is: What comes next?

You should recognize the pattern as one involving rotation. The arrow is slowly turning around an axis.

The answer is: A position of the arrow. Because the arrow rotates 45° to the right with each movement, the next movement will bring it to this position: ↓.

How to Practice Recognizing Translations, Rotations, and Reflections

Write a capital letter at the top of a sheet of paper. Below it, write the same letter in a row with two or more other letters, and have the child circle the one that is the same as the one at the top. Continue with other letters. Try to include as distractors (wrong choices) letters that are similar in shape to the letter you chose.

Example:

```
          A                      P
   R    V   (A)          R    (P)    D
```

Have children write a lowercase *b* and rotate or reflect it to end up with the letters *p, q,* and *d.* Challenge them to find which capital letters can be reflected horizontally or vertically with no apparent change (H, I, O, and X).

Place a spoon on the table. Rotate it 90° to the right. Have children show where it will end up with another such rotation. Continue with turns to the left, turns of 45°, turns of 180°, and so on. As an alternative, have children predict how many turns of a given sort it will take to get the spoon back to its original position.

Example:

The next turn will bring it to this position:

Two more turns will bring it to the original position.

 Use a fork, a small mirror, and a piece of paper. Place the fork on the table where it can be seen in the mirror. Have children note which way the fork is pointing on the table, and which way it is pointing in the mirror. Cover the mirror with the paper, place the fork in a different position, and have children describe which way they expect it to point in the mirror. Remove the paper to check their guess. Continue with other positions.

Example:

Focus on
Difficult Concepts
(Grades 4 and Up)

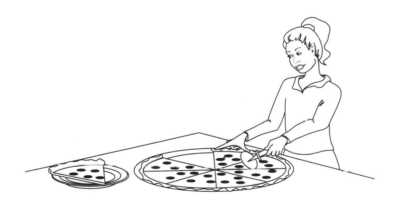

46.

Fractions

What is $\frac{1}{4}$ of $\frac{1}{2}$?

What is $\frac{1}{2}$ divided by $\frac{1}{4}$?

Fractions are incredibly useful, but they often prove difficult for children to master. Usually, the reason is that numbers are thrown at children without adequate attention to what those numbers mean.

Much about fractions seems to go against common sense. For example, why should $\frac{1}{8}$ be less than $\frac{1}{7}$ when 8 is greater than 7? Why should $\frac{1}{5} \times \frac{1}{6}$ equal a fraction less than $\frac{1}{5}$ or $\frac{1}{6}$, when multiplying 5×6 yields a number greater than 5 or 6? And why is there so much new language to learn: *numerator, denominator, reciprocal?* It's little wonder that many children who have moved blithely through whole-number concepts lose their minds briefly when they encounter fractions.

You can help your child understand fractions by relating the numbers to real things. Don't worry about the vocabulary of fractions. Think: "$\frac{1}{2}$ means one out of two." It might mean one object in a set of two, or it might mean one part out of two parts.

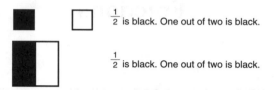

$\frac{1}{2}$ is black. One out of two is black.

$\frac{1}{2}$ is black. One out of two is black.

If you think in real object terms about fractions, a problem like the one that opens this chapter starts to make sense.

You know that: $\frac{1}{2}$ means one out of two.

The question is: What is $\frac{1}{4}$ of $\frac{1}{2}$?

Suppose you start with the picture of the square shown earlier. The black section represents one out of two parts. You need to show one out of four parts of that. You could do that by cutting that black section $\left(\frac{1}{2}\right)$ into four equal parts $\left(\frac{1}{4}\right)$. Keep in mind that the denominator tells you how many equal parts to split something into, and the numerator tells you how many parts to consider.

The answer is: A fraction of the whole. Since you could make 8 sections the size of the one you just made, the section you made is one out of 8, or $\frac{1}{8}$.

$\frac{1}{2}$ is black. One out of two is black.

$\frac{1}{4}$ of that $\frac{1}{2}$ is $\frac{1}{8}$ of the whole.

One of the least obvious concepts in all of mathematics is what happens when you divide a fraction. When you divide a whole number by a whole number, you wind up with a smaller number. When you divide a fraction by a fraction, you wind up with a larger number, which seems to contradict the meaning of *divide* entirely. One problem with dividing fractions is that there's rarely any reason to do so in real life.

You know that: $\frac{1}{2}$ means one out of two.

The question is: What is $\frac{1}{2}$ divided by $\frac{1}{4}$?

You can use the strategy Find an Easier Problem (see #37) to rethink this problem. What if you plugged in some whole numbers instead?

What is 4 divided by 2?

To solve this easier problem, you know that you're really finding how many 2s there are in 4. So think about the fraction question the same way: How many $\frac{1}{4}$s are there in $\frac{1}{2}$?

The answer is: A number of $\frac{1}{4}$ parts. Since you can fit two $\frac{1}{4}$ parts into one $\frac{1}{2}$ part, the answer is <u>2</u>.

$\frac{1}{2}$ is black. One out of two is black.

There are 2 $\frac{1}{4}$ s in that black section.

The most common use of fractions is in measurement, and that is where you can best show children how fractions work. You've seen some indications of how to use cooking, home repair, and crafts to interest children in math (see #2, #3, and #4). Here are some specific suggestions for using fractions in the home.

How to Practice Using Fractions

Use a 1-cup measuring cup. Have younger children show you $\frac{1}{2}$ cup of water, $\frac{1}{4}$ cup of water, $\frac{1}{3}$ cup of water, and so on. Ask older children to show you the same amounts and then to show you $\frac{1}{2}$ of $\frac{1}{2}$ (fill the cup to $\frac{1}{2}$ and pour out $\frac{1}{2}$ of that), $\frac{1}{2}$ of $\frac{1}{4}$, and $\frac{1}{2}$ of $\frac{1}{3}$. Point out that the children can count the markings on the side of the cup to help them find the exact answer.

Display a ruler or measuring tape. Ask children to count the divisions in 1 inch and name the fraction for each mark on the ruler or tape. Older children should be able to name fractions in reduced terms ($\frac{1}{4}$ instead of $\frac{4}{16}$, for example).

Example:

There are 16 marks. The fractions from 0 to 1 are $\frac{1}{16}$, $\frac{2}{16}$ or $\frac{1}{8}$, $\frac{3}{16}$, $\frac{4}{16}$ or $\frac{1}{4}$, $\frac{5}{16}$, $\frac{6}{16}$ or $\frac{3}{8}$, $\frac{7}{16}$, $\frac{8}{16}$ or $\frac{1}{2}$, $\frac{9}{16}$, $\frac{10}{16}$ or $\frac{5}{8}$, $\frac{11}{16}$, $\frac{12}{16}$ or $\frac{3}{4}$, $\frac{13}{16}$, $\frac{14}{16}$ or $\frac{7}{8}$, $\frac{15}{16}$, $\frac{16}{16}$ or 1.

Now have children put the ruler away and challenge them to draw lines that are $\frac{1}{2}$ inch, 2 inches, and $5\frac{1}{4}$ inches long. Have them check their answers with a ruler and use subtraction to determine how far off their guesses were.

Example:

My 2-inch line was really $2\frac{5}{8}$ inches long.
$2\frac{5}{8} - 2 = \frac{5}{8}$, so I was $\frac{5}{8}$ inches off.

Have children use a ruler to measure a book cover. Tell them to use whatever means they like to determine the measurements of a book exactly twice as long and wide as that one, three times as long and wide, and half as long and wide. Then have them find other books on their shelves and estimate their measurements, based on the measurements they've already determined. They can use their rulers to check their guesses.

47.

Percents

Sales tax in your area is 7%. If you have $20 and are purchasing a CD that costs $17.95, will you have enough money to pay for the CD?

Many adults feel so uncomfortable with percents that they'll overtip a delivery person, postpone refinancing a mortgage, and blindly pay an incorrectly calculated credit card bill just to avoid dealing with the concept. When I first moved to New York, I remember sitting in cabs and recalculating the tip every time the meter clicked simply out of panic that I wouldn't be fast enough when the cab actually stopped at my destination. It's a weird phobia; although percents are a form of fractions, they're really much easier to calculate than most fractions are.

Percent, of course, means "per hundred." The way we use percents, we're usually talking about dollars and cents. When we say 7 percent, we mean "7 out of 100," which in monetary terms means "7 cents out of each dollar." Percents are always parts "of" something, so you can usually use multiplication (the operation of "of") to solve a percent problem.

So look back at the earlier problem:

You know that: You have $20, and the CD costs $17.95. Sales tax is 7%.
The question is: Will $20 take care of the CD plus tax?

The first thing to do is to find an easier number to deal with than $17.95. Rounding it up to $18 makes sense—if you have enough money to pay for an $18 CD, you have enough to pay for one that costs 5 cents less.

If sales tax is 7 percent, that means that for every dollar an item costs, you really spend 7 cents more. For an item that costs $18, you spend 18 times 7 cents more, or $1.26.

The answer is: Either yes or no. The CD costs around $18, and your tax is $1.26, so $18 + $1.26 = $19.26. <u>Yes</u>, you will have enough money.

Percent problems involving 1 percent and 10 percent and 100 percent are easy, because they merely require moving the decimal point two, one, or zero places.

Example:
Start with the dollar amount $32.00.

1% of $32.00	=	$.32
10% of $32.00	=	$3.20
100% of $32.00	=	$32.00

A good way to think of other percents is in terms of these easier percent problems. For example, 7% = 7 × 1%; 70% = 7 × 10%. The only way to become really comfortable with percents is to practice using them.

How to Practice Using Percents

Try some practical life-skill problem solving. Save the junk mail you receive that advertises credit cards at various rates and fees. Have your children help you calculate the interest on a $100 purchase for each card and determine which is the best deal.

Similarly, you might get bank brochures from local banks and have children help you decide where it makes the most sense to keep the college fund: in a savings account, a certificate of deposit, a savings bond, or some other type of investment.

Use my old system the next time you're in a city cab together. Ask children to recalculate the tip block by block or minute by minute.

At a restaurant, challenge children to choose a selection that, with your local percent tax and a 15 percent tip, will total under $5, $10, or an amount of your choosing.

Different states have different tax rates. Give children your receipts from the mall and have them determine what you would have paid had the tax rate been 1 percent less, or what you would have paid if every item were tax-free.

48.

Ratios and Proportions

You have a favorite 3" × 5" photo you want blown up to
8" × 10" size. Will you lose any details in the enlargement?

A *ratio* is a means of comparing numbers. Ratios are often recorded as fractions; for example, the ratio 2 to 3 might be written $\frac{2}{3}$. It might also be written 2:3.

A *proportion* is usually an equation stating that two ratios are equal. The ratio $\frac{2}{3}$ is equal to the ratio $\frac{4}{6}$. In other words, if you have a photo that measures 2" × 3" and blow it up to measure 4" × 6", nothing is lost; the two photos are in proportion.

Unfortunately, most photo shops give you a choice of 3" × 5", 4" × 6", 5" × 7", and 8" × 10". You can see at a glance that

$$\frac{3}{5} \neq \frac{4}{6} \neq \frac{5}{7} \neq \frac{8}{10}$$

Therefore, any time you move from one size to the next, you lose something from the horizontal or vertical field of the original photo.

The easiest way to solve proportions is to *cross-multiply,* a term that you may remember vaguely from school:

$$\frac{3}{5} \bowtie \frac{8}{10} \qquad 3 \times 10 = 30 \qquad\qquad 5 \times 8 = 40$$

The cross products are not equal,
so the proportion is false.

In a true proportion such as $\frac{2}{3} = \frac{4}{6}$, the cross products will always be equal. The reason is that $\frac{2}{3}$ and $\frac{4}{6}$ name the same number; you simply multiply $\frac{2}{3}$ by 1 in the form of $\frac{2}{3}$ to get $\frac{4}{6}$.*

---

*Note: The proof of this goes as follows and is referred to as "The product of the means equals the product of the extremes," where the means are the inside terms b and c and the extremes are the outside terms a and d in the proportion a:b = c:d. As you've seen, that proportion may also be written this way:

$$\frac{a}{b} = \frac{c}{d}$$

Because any number times 1 equals itself, you could then state that

$$\frac{c}{d} = \frac{a}{b} \times \frac{x}{x}$$

Multiplying both sides by the inverse, or reciprocal, of one of the ratios gives you

$$\frac{b}{a} \times \frac{c}{d} = \frac{a}{b} \times \frac{x}{x} \times \frac{b}{a}$$

Any number times its reciprocal equals 1, so you can cancel out the reciprocals on the right side of the equal sign and end up with

$$\frac{b}{a} \times \frac{c}{d} = \frac{x}{x}$$

To multiply fractions, you multiply the numerators and then the denominators. Any fraction $\frac{x}{x}$ is equal to 1. Therefore,

$$\frac{bc}{ad} = 1$$

If a fraction is equal to 1, its numerator must equal its denominator. So

$$bc = ad$$

In school, if not in real life, children will face questions like these: What percent of 25 is 2?

2 is 25% of what number?

You can solve these kinds of problems in many ways, but I find it easiest to think about them in terms of ratios, keeping in mind that *percent* always means "out of 100."

$$\frac{2}{25} = \frac{x}{100} \qquad \frac{2}{x} = \frac{25}{100}$$

You then cross-multiply and divide to solve:

$2 \times 100 = 25x$

$200 \div 25 = 8$

So 2 is <u>8%</u> of 25.   So 2 is 25% of <u>8</u>.

Ratios and proportions are a simple way to solve many of the problems in this book. The first problem in #34, for example, can be solved by thinking:

$$\frac{\$2.55}{3\,\text{wks}} = \frac{\$x}{1\,\text{wk}} \quad x = \underline{\$.85}$$

The problem in #36 might be solved with a proportion as well:

$$\frac{\$147,630}{3,700\,\text{sq.ft.}} < \frac{\$124,750}{2,500\,\text{sq.ft.}}$$

Being able to handle proportions provides you with a shortcut to the solution of all kinds of problems.

Ratios are especially useful in cooking and arts and crafts (see #2 and #4). Here are some ways to familiarize children with the concept of ratios.

How to Practice Using Ratios and Proportions

✐ Dig out a home furnishings catalog and have children determine whether certain items that come in various sizes—rugs and sheets, for example—are in proportion from size to size. In other words, is a 5" × 8" rug proportional to one that measures 9" × 12"? How can you tell?

✐ Practice drawing from nature by thinking in terms of proportions. As an example, display a flower to draw, and point out the proportions yourself—"the stem is twice as long as the leaves, the petals seem to be $\frac{1}{3}$ the size of the leaves," and so on. Children might like to draw on graph paper, which can help them make more accurate measurements.

✐ Have children measure their head circumferences and their waists and express the result as a ratio. Measure your own and have children determine whether the resulting ratios are proportional. If you have smaller children, it might be fun to compare their ratios to your own as well.

✐ If you have children's furniture or dollhouse furniture in the house, have children measure a chair or table and express its relation to the measurement of a normal-sized chair or table in terms of a ratio. Is the small chair proportional to the large chair in width, length, *and* height?

49.

Negative Numbers

When you last looked at the thermometer, it read 10°. Now it reads ⁻10°. How many degrees has it dropped?

If ever there's a time to use the Draw a Picture or Diagram strategy (see #40), it's when you first deal with negative numbers. Much of the difficulty children have when they meet negative numbers (usually around the sixth or seventh grade) comes from the fact that they can't visualize them. It's easy to picture 10—children have been doing that since preschool—10 fingers, 10 cents, 10 blocks. But how do you picture ⁻10?

The problem with negative numbers is that they name values rather than amounts of objects. The only way to picture them is in linear terms. In a football game, you can gain yards, or you can lose yards. *Negative yardage* refers to a loss. It's not difficult to picture a football field with a ball moving forward (in a positive direction) and being brought back (for negative yardage).

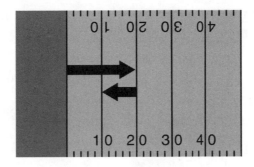

This represents a gain of 20 yards followed by a loss of 10.

You might also picture a thermometer with numbers ranging from below zero to above zero. By simple counting, you can solve the problem presented earlier.

You know that: It was 10°. It's now ⁻10°.

The question is: How many degrees has it dropped?

Count the marks from 10 to ⁻10. Because each mark stands for 2°, it's easy to find the answer by counting by 2s.

The answer is: An amount of degrees. Because it's an amount that's asked for, not a value, the number must be positive. By counting marks, you can see that the answer is <u>20</u>.

Drawing a number line helps when you're comparing numbers, adding numbers, or subtracting numbers.

The Draw a Picture or Diagram strategy is almost useless, however, when it comes to multiplying and dividing with negative numbers. Usually, children are told to memorize the rules: *Positive times positive is positive; positive times negative is negative; negative times negative is positive.* The easiest way to make sense of these operations is to look for patterns in sets of multiplication problems:

$3 \times 2 = 6$ $2 \times {}^-3 = {}^-6$

$3 \times 1 = 3$ $1 \times {}^-3 = {}^-3$

$3 \times 0 = 0$ $0 \times {}^-3 = 0$

$3 \times {}^-1 = {}^-3$ ${}^-1 \times {}^-3 = 3$

$3 \times {}^-2 = {}^-6$ ${}^-2 \times {}^-3 = 6$

Keeping in mind that you check multiplication by dividing (the two are inverse operations), you can use these same problems to prove division rules too: *Positive divided by positive is positive; positive divided by negative is negative; negative divided by positive is negative; negative divided by negative is positive.*

$6 \div 2 = 3$ $^-6 \div {}^-2 = 3$

$^-6 \div 2 = {}^-3$ $6 \div {}^-2 = {}^-3$

Here's a cute mnemonic my friend Chantal taught me:

Multiplication or Division	Good Guys (+)	Bad Guys (–)
To town (+)	+	–
Away from town (–)	–	+

In other words, when the good guys (+) come to town (+), it's a good situation (+). When the bad guys (–) go away from town (–), it's a good situation (+), and so on.

How to Practice Using Negative Numbers

With younger children, play a "Simon Says" game that involves taking steps forward and back. Give commands such as "move positive three" for forward movement and "move negative three" for backward movement.

Draw a number line in chalk on the sidewalk. Have it range from $^-10$ to $^+10$. Have children act out addition and subtraction of signed numbers by walking through the problems on the chalk number line.

Example: $4 + {}^-6 = ?$

The child starts at 0 and moves up 4 to show the first number to be added. Then he or she moves back 6, to end at $^-2$.

Ask children to keep a temperature diary for a week, recording the temperature each day and referring to the change from day to day in terms of a positive or negative number.

Show children how to record credits and debits (money received and money spent) as positive and negative numbers. Suggest that they keep track of their allowances and expenditures by using this method.

50.

Probability

You toss a die in hopes of getting a 3 and winning the game. What is the probability your toss will be a 3?

John Allen Paulos, author of the best-seller *Innumeracy,* devotes much of his text to discussion of how people who don't understand math (people who are *innumerate*) are constantly fooled by statistics. They live in fear of terrorist attacks, airplane crashes, and other disasters simply because they don't understand probability.

The probability of any event may be expressed as the number of favorable outcomes over the number of possible outcomes. If you toss a die in hopes of getting a 3, your odds are

$\dfrac{1}{6}$ (favorable outcome = 3 pips)
(possible outcomes on a six-sided die)

Other ways of stating this are "one in six" or "one out of six." On the other hand, the odds of tossing a 7 are $\frac{0}{6}$—the event is impossible. The odds of tossing a number from 1 to 6 are $\frac{6}{6}$—the event is certain. The odds of tossing a 3 or a 4 are $\frac{2}{6}$, and so on.

Suppose you toss two dice. Because the outcome of tossing the first has no effect on the outcome of tossing the second, we call these *independent events*. To find the probability of tossing a 3 on *both* dice, you multiply the probability of the first event times the probability of the second.

$$\frac{1}{6} \times \frac{1}{6} = \frac{1}{36}$$

Therefore, the probability of being in an airline crash caused by a terrorist attack is even smaller than the probability of being in one or the other. Understanding probability helps us understand voter polls, health statistics, sports analyses, and product reports (see #16 and #17). It helps us differentiate random events from predictable events and determine the likelihood of those predictable events, which can, in turn, ease our irrational fears of the world.

How to Practice Using Probability

As children help you fold laundry, have them determine the probability of forming a pair of socks by choosing two loose socks at random. Point out that as pairs are made successfully and set aside, the probability goes up because the number of possible outcomes goes down.

Play guessing games: "I'm thinking of a letter from A to Z. What is it?" Discuss the probability of getting the answer correct on the first try $\left(\frac{1}{26}\right)$, on the second try $\left(\frac{1}{25}\right)$, because you eliminated one possible outcome with the first try), and so on. Change the game to "a number from 1 to 10," "a number from 1 to 50," "a letter from A to G," "the name of a member of our family," and so on.

Play games with checkers and a paper bag. Have children use black and red checkers to show what checkers you should start with to have a 1 in 5 chance of choosing a black one, a 3 in 5 chance of choosing a red one, and so on. Then try the experiment by placing the checkers in a bag and drawing one checker at random.

91A 5351

LOTTERY: A TAX ON PEOPLE
WHO ARE BAD AT MATH

M860-TN
20 R